Laurent Tirard
MOVIEMAKERS' MASTER CLASS

Laurent Tirard was born in 1967. He studied filmmaking at New York University, from which he graduated with honors in 1989. After a year as a script reader for the Warner Bros. studio in Los Angeles, he became a journalist for the French film magazine *Studio*. There, over the course of seven years, he screened and reviewed more than a hundred films per year. He also had the opportunity to interview all the great directors of the day, including Martin Scorsese, Jean-Luc Godard, John Woo, Steven Spielberg, Woody Allen, and many others, engaging them in lengthy discussions on the most practical aspects of filmmaking for a series called *Leçons de Cinéma*. For the last four years, he has put all his lessons into practice, first as a screenwriter on French features and TV movies, then as the director of two short films, *Reliable Sources* and *Tomorrow Is Another Day*. The first received the 1999 Panavision Award at the Avignon/New York Film Festival; the second was selected for the 2000 Telluride Film Festival. Laurent Tirard is currently working on his first feature film as a director. He lives in Paris with his wife and son.

Moviemakers' Master Class

MOVIEMAKERS' MASTER CLASS

Private Lessons from

the World's Foremost

Directors

LAURENT TIRARD

FABER AND FABER
New York ■ London

Faber and Faber, Inc.
An affiliate of Farrar, Straus and Giroux
19 Union Square West, New York 10003

Faber and Faber Ltd.
3 Queen Square
London WC1N 3AU

Photo credits appear on p. 217.

This book has not been been prepared, authorized, licensed, approved, or endorsed by the publishers of **MovieMaker" Magazine**.

Library of Congress Cataloging-in-Publication Data
Tirard, Laurent, 1967–
    Moviemakers' master class : private lessons from the world's
foremost directors / by Laurent Tirard.— 1st ed.
        p.   cm.
    Chiefly a collection of interviews originally published in
French in Studio, 1996–2000.
    Contents: Groundbreakers: John Boorman, Sydney Pollack,
Claude Sautet —Revisionists: Woody Allen, Bernardo
Bertolucci, Martin Scorsese, Wim Wenders — Dream weavers:
Pedro Almodóvar, Tim Burton, David Cronenberg, Jean-
Pierre Jeunet, David Lynch — Big guns: Oliver Stone, John
Woo — New blood: Joel and Ethan Coen, Takeshi Kitano, Emir
Justurica, Lars Von Trier, Wong Kar-wai — In a class of his own:
Jean-Luc Godard.
    ISBN-13: 978-0-571-21102-9
    ISBN-10: 0-571-21102-X (pbk. : alk. paper)
    1. Motion pictures—Production and direction.   2. Motion
picture producers and directors—Interviews.   I. Title.
PN1995.9.P7 T495 2002
791.43'0233—dc21

                                                        2002019927

Designed by Debbie Glasserman

www.fsgbooks.com

14   13   12   11   10   9   8   7   6   5

To Ben Sims, a teacher who became a friend, a mentor, and, in many ways, a second father

To my grandfather Albert Desmedt, a journalist who kept hoping that I would follow in his footsteps but who, unfortunately, did not live to see his wish come to pass

And, of course, to all the filmmakers who have dazzled me over the years (even though their talent has often inhibited me as much as it has inspired me!). Most of them are in this book. The others should expect to hear from me soon . . .

Contents

BIG GUNS

NEW BLOOD

IN A CLASS BY HIMSELF

Preface

In December 1995, *Studio* magazine asked me to interview a young director named James Gray, whose first film, *Little Odessa*, had really impressed me. Though a little standoffish at first, James turned out to be a very talkative, extremely articulate person. The one hour he had originally granted me quickly turned into a pleasant three-hour lunch. As we were about to part, I asked him what he was currently working on. He answered that he was slowly writing a new screenplay—which would eventually become a film he made five years later, *The Yards*—but that his main activity was teaching filmmaking to first-year students at UCLA.

I will admit that my first reaction was jealousy. Eight years earlier, I had entered the New York University Film School with the naïve hope that some of the famous directors who had graduated from the school—Martin Scorsese, Oliver Stone, Joel and Ethan Coen—would drop in and teach us a few things, or at least give a lecture once in a while. But it never happened. I had great teachers, and I am grateful for all the support and inspiration they gave me. Still, I wish I had been able to take at least one class with someone whose films I had seen and admired and whose knowledge would necessarily have been more specific and pragmatic. Which is why the idea that some fortunate UCLA freshmen were being introduced to filmmaking by someone like James Gray made me more than a little envious.

As I went back home after that interview, I had the crazy idea of asking James if I could come and sit through his class for a whole semester, take notes, and then publish a summary of it in the magazine. I doubt that James would have agreed, and I know *Studio* would quite rightly have refused to let me do such a project. But the thought stayed with me all the same.

I should explain that, at the time, I was desperately trying to make a change in my professional life. I had not originally set out to become a journalist. I wanted to make films. And so, after I graduated from NYU, I went straight to Hollywood, certain that the big studios would soon be begging me to direct their next blockbuster. Needless to say, *I* ended up doing all the begging—and was very grateful when I finally landed a job as a low-ranking script reader. Most of the screenplays I went through were terrible. The good ones, however, were so well written that I quickly realized I was light-years away from making my own films. I just didn't have the maturity—maybe I didn't have the talent either. But let's brush aside that possibility for the moment.

As my illusions were quickly fading away, I met one of the editors of *Studio* magazine, a high-end French film publication, who offered me a job as a critic. Though the prospect of getting paid to watch movies all year long was tempting, I was very hesitant. My parents had always told me, in a way they thought was reassuring, that if I failed as a filmmaker, I could always become a film critic. And even though I was perfectly willing to make a detour on the way to my ultimate goal, I did not want to get stuck in a professional dead end. But I took the job anyway, and it turned out to be a better move than I could have imagined. I learned to watch films in a more analytical way and became better at communicating what I liked or disliked about them. Best of all, I eventually got to interview people I had never imagined I could even meet—at least, not while I was awake.

Yet I was still a filmmaker at heart. And after several years spent *watching* films, something told me it was time to make my way back to *making* them.

To say that I was a little scared at the prospect of leaving a secure job to leap back into the unknown world of independent filmmaking would be an understatement: I was petrified. It had been ten years since I had made a short film. The lessons of film school were long gone, and I missed the guidance and reassurance of my instructors. I needed to refresh my framework, to find a teacher who would take me through the basics again. It was at this juncture that I was sent to interview James Gray.

After that encounter, it dawned on me that I was actually in the ideal situation to refresh—and perfect—my entire understanding of film. Until then, I had always approached my job from a purely journalistic point of view. But I now realized that I could also approach it as a filmmaker. Instead of asking directors questions they had already been asked a hundred times—questions along the lines of "So what was it like working with this or that actress? Is she the same in real life as in your film?"—why not ask more pragmatic questions, such as "How do you decide where to set the camera for a given shot?" A very basic question, granted—but a crucial one.

I decided to create a series of interviews called *Cinema Lessons (Leçons de Cinéma)* and convinced the editors of *Studio* magazine to give it a try. I was a little worried that *Studio's* readers, who obviously bought the magazine for its glamorous approach to movies—encompassing glossy pictures and lengthy star interviews—might find my approach too technical and obscure. But driven, I confess, by the self-serving aspect of my enterprise, I quickly shrugged these doubts away. And so I proceeded to design a set of about twenty basic questions to pose to a diverse group of talented filmmakers. I asked questions as existential as "Do you make a film to express certain concrete ideas, or is the film a way for you to find out what you want to say?" and as pragmatic as "How do you decide on camera angles?"

I was tempted to ask different questions of different directors, tailoring the interviews to each of them. But I have come to understand that this would have been a mistake. Indeed, it quickly became clear that the most fascinating aspect of the series was showing that a hundred directors have a hundred different ways of making a film—and that all of them are right. The lesson of all these interviews is really that one has to create one's own approach to filmmaking. A young filmmaker may love Lars Von Trier's visual style but feel more comfortable with the way Woody Allen directs actors. It is possible to use both their styles and blend them into something that is entirely new.

Choosing the directors I wanted to interview was easy. Putting aside issues of personal taste, there were a large number of filmmakers whose work and experience made them obvious candidates, and I quickly made a list with more than seventy names on it. The hard part was to reserve time in the schedules of these overworked directors. In fact, the only time a journalist can get them to sit down for an hour and answer questions is when they have to promote a film. So if you're wondering how I selected the twenty-one filmmakers in this book from my original list of seventy, I am tempted to answer that they are simply the first twenty-one who walked through the door. More accurately, they are the first twenty-one filmmakers who came to Paris with their new films.

Promotional schedules are tight, and I rarely had more

than an hour scheduled with any director, though sometimes I managed to get two hours. Time constraints were frustrating. At the same time, these directors have mastered their craft so fully that they were able to answer my questions with impressive speed. Woody Allen, for instance, finished the whole interview in a dizzying thirty minutes. He answered my questions so thoroughly and so quickly that I almost suspected someone had slipped them to him beforehand. In any case, almost every word he said ended up in the final text, which should give you a good idea of how precise he was.

Readers of *Studio* magazine greatly enjoyed the interviews—and wrote letters saying so. Contrary to my initial fears about being too specialized, it seems that these "master classes" appealed to average filmgoers who wanted more information on how the films they see are made. I think they also appreciated the conciseness of the format. To a purist—or serious film student—it was perhaps unthinkable that a director's thought process could be conveyed in fewer than five hundred pages. But ordinary mortals—like myself—do not always have time to read a massive volume on every filmmaker they find intriguing.

The directors enjoyed the interviews too. They were happy to escape the tediousness of their promotional duties for a while to discuss the very core of their craft. Some of them joked that I was stealing all their little secrets, but they all went along with the process gladly, and they were usually curious to read the final edited interview. No director ever disappointed me—except one. He, who must remain anonymous and who is notorious for his wild lifestyle, kept falling asleep during the interview! And when he was awake, his answers were so far off the topic that I had to scratch the entire piece.

I also have two regrets. The first is that I did not have an opportunity to interview Samuel Fuller, who lived in Paris for several years before returning to Los Angeles, where he died in 1997. The second is that, ironically, I haven't yet had the opportunity to interview James Gray, who is obviously at the top of my list since he was my initial inspiration for the series. James came to France in 2000 to show *The Yards* at the Cannes Film Festival, but unfortunately, I was not there at the time.

What have been my most rewarding moments? Two come immediately to mind. The first was when Jean-Pierre Jeunet told me that he had read David Lynch's interview and had tried to put some of Lynch's ideas into practice while shooting *Alien Resurrection*. And the second was when Tim Burton finally asked the magic question: "Are you going to make this into a book eventually?"

Strangely, until that moment, the idea of putting all these interviews into book form had not occurred to me (probably because, as I've hinted, I'm a reluctant reader myself). Truth be told, I never opened any of the books on film theory that we were assigned in film school. In spite of that, the idea of making a book out of all my interviews was pretty exciting. But how would I go about it? I didn't have a clue.

A few months after my conversation with Tim Burton, I was invited to the Avignon Film Festival by Jerry Rudes, the Texas-born founder and director of the event, who has been running this "crossroads of French and American cinema" for many years in the south of France. If you haven't heard about the festival, it's probably because the people who have been there enjoyed it so much that they try to keep it a secret. The town is beautiful, the staff treats you like family, the films are great, and Jerry's amazing energy draws the best out of people. At one point during one of the sun-soaked, wine-drenched days of screenings and seminars, I asked Jerry what he did the rest of the year. And as luck would have it, he told me that he worked with the Fifi Oscard Agency in New York, trying to get interesting manuscripts about film published. Thanks to Jerry and Fifi Oscard, my interviews were put into the form of a book proposal, which was eventually purchased for publication by Faber and Faber, Inc.

To backtrack just a little, I should explain that I originally went to the Avignon Film Festival to show a short film I had directed. Over the last three years, I have made two shorts. With an enormous amount of luck, I might finally get to direct a feature within the not-too-distant future. I mention all this not to sound conceited but because I would like to conclude by reflecting on what these interviews have brought me as a filmmaker.

First of all, they gave me the confidence to see there are scores of ways to make a film. Everyone can approach filmmaking in his or her own way; in fact, everyone should. All you need is a point of view, instinct, and determination. Talent comes into play as well, but not necessarily to the extent that most people think. For example, no matter how brilliant and articulate Jean-Luc Godard and Martin Scorsese are about how and why they make films, they did not wake up one morning with their amazing knowledge. They acquired it through years of hard-earned experience. That is what I have tried to present in this book through each filmmaker's quite pragmatic master class.

The advice of all these directors came in particularly handy when I started to direct my own short films. In the first one, for example, I had to direct nine actors in the same scene, and I was glad I could draw on Sydney Pollack's advice to never give an actor directions in front of other actors. When I was preparing my second film, which was essentially about two friends drifting apart, I remembered what John Boorman had said about using the wide-screen format (Cinemascope) to create a physical relationship between the actors in the frame

that would work as a metaphor of their emotional relationship. I then decided to shoot the film in wide screen. It might
have seemed illogical, given the claustrophobic nature of the
story, but it worked beautifully.

To me, these master classes are timesaving devices. I use
them like a checklist before I make a film to see if some of the
advice can help me solve problems on the shoot I'm preparing. And even though I now consider myself a filmmaker and
not a journalist anymore, I will continue to pursue the directors on my list for these specialized interviews because I am
still amazed at the number of things I learn each time I speak
to one of the masters. I hope you, the reader, find these lessons as inspiring and as useful as I have, whether you're also
trying to make films or just looking for a more insightful way
to watch them.

Laurent Tirard
Paris
June 2001

Acknowledgments

The author wishes to thank:

Studio magazine, particularly Jean-Pierre Lavoignat, Christophe D'Yvoire, Pascaline Baudoin, Benjamin Plet, and Françoise D'Inca;

all the PR people who made the interviews possible: Michèle Abitbol, Denise Breton, Michel Burnstein, Claude Davy, Françoise Dessaigne, Marquita Doassans, François Frey, François Guerar, Laurence Hartman-Churlaud, Vanessa Jerrom, Jerôme Jouneaux, Anne Lara, Marie-Christine Malbert, Marie Queysane, Robert Schlokoff, and Jean-Pierre Vincent;

the Cinemathèque de Nice (which arranged the interviews with Claude Sautet and Sydney Pollack);

the Locarno Film Festival (which arranged the interview with Bernardo Bertolucci);

Ian Burley, who translated all the French interviews into English;

all the filmmakers' assistants who handled my requests for legal paperwork;

and, finally, Jerry Rudes and the Fifi Oscard Agency.

GROUNDBREAKERS

John Boorman
Sydney Pollack
Claude Sautet

The title of this section might make the reader think that these three directors have a conventional approach to filmmaking. Nothing could be more untrue. However, with the exception of Jean-Luc Godard (whose interview appears in the last section), these are the only directors in the book who started their careers before the cultural upheavals of the late sixties, and thus probably are the ones who started out in the most conservative environment. For them, breaking out of the mold of tradition and finding a personal voice were certainly harder tasks than they were for directors of the generations that followed. These directors became auteurs at a time when that notion didn't yet exist.

JOHN BOORMAN

b. 1933, London, England

Though I had never met John Boorman before interviewing him, actors from his films whom I had interviewed all agreed that he was the nicest man they'd ever worked with. He is, indeed, someone who immediately makes you feel comfortable. Boorman seems particularly tranquil and looks as though he could deal with any situation, however catastrophic, with a shrug and a smile. We met at the time that The General *was being released, in 1998. I tried to compliment him on the film but did it so clumsily that I think he got the wrong idea. I said if I hadn't seen his name on the credits, I would have thought the film had been directed by a twenty-year-old. He seemed perplexed by that remark, but what I had meant was that I found it amazing that after all these years of directing films, he could still exhibit the freshness to make one so modern.*

Starting as a director in 1965, John Boorman has always tried—sometimes without success, it is true—to explore all forms of cinema, from the experimental genre film Point Blank *to the revisionist operatic epic* Excalibur. *Thanks to our conversation, I now know what it was that made his version of the Arthurian legend somehow more ambiguous and more exciting than other cinematic interpretations.*

We talked for an hour. Boorman visibly enjoyed getting down to explaining the nitty-gritty of his job, but at the end of the interview, he suddenly frowned and said, "Wait a minute. You just stole all my little secrets here!" Then he shrugged and smiled, wishing me luck.

■ Master Class with John Boorman

I learned filmmaking in a very organic way. I started as a film critic when I was eighteen, writing reviews for a newspaper. Then I got a job as a trainee film editor, then as an editor, then I began to direct documentaries for the BBC. After a while, I became dissatisfied with documentaries, and I began to dramatize them more and more, until I started doing dramas for TV and, eventually, for the cinema. So it was really organic and natural, and what helped in all the documentaries that I did was really the fact of shooting so much film, and the familiarity that this created with the process of filming. For me, technique became something that I never worried about. It was there even before I shot my first film. I never had to struggle with it. I know most directors now go to film schools, but I'm not a big believer in that system. I think filmmaking is essentially a practical undertaking, and I think that the apprenticeship system has always been the most effective. I mean, theory is interesting, but it is only interesting when it's related to practical work. And my experience with film students is that they're quite impractical when it comes to the pragmatic aspect of filmmaking. I have, however, helped young directors make their first movies. I produced Neil Jordan's first film, for instance, which in effect was a tutoring operation.

When you're preparing a film with a young director, I find the most important thing to teach him, which often even experienced directors fail to do, is to honestly time the script. Now, most people start out making a picture which is too long. And in consequence, if you end up with a first cut that is three hours long, and you've got to get down to two hours, it means that one-third of the time that you spent shooting the film was wasted, because you spent that time on scenes that won't eventually get in the picture. Of course, it's always important to have a little extra, a few scenes that you can cut into or eliminate if they don't work. But in most cases, you lie to yourself. You're not honest about how long it's going to be because you can't bear to go back to the script and make sacrifices. To do this, however, the best method is to work it out when you're scheduling the shoot. That scene needs fourteen shots? OK, that's two days. Is that scene really worth two days of shooting? If the answer is no, then what you have to do is rewrite the scene or cut it out. This way, you look at the resources, you look at the money you have to spend on the film, and you look at the time and effort that are going to be devoted to each scene, and you can judge whether it has that value or not.

ALL DIRECTORS WRITE

Directing is really about writing, and all serious directors write. They might not get credit for it, often for contractual reasons, but I think you can't separate the shaping of the script from the writing of it. And I think all serious directors shape their scripts, meaning that they sit down with the writers and put the ideas into shape and give them structure. It's an essential part of directing. To which you have to add the whole process of interpretation and exploration. I make films to explore. If I don't know what a film is about, I go on to make it. Whereas if I know exactly what it's about, then I will lose interest in it. So it is the excitement of exploration which appeals to me, and the danger that's involved in that, and you always hope that it's going to lead you into something really new, fresh, and original. The only moment when I know what a film is about is when I've seen it with an audience. And there are always surprises. When I made *Hope and Glory*, which is about my childhood memories, it wasn't until I saw it finished that I realized that my obsession with the Arthurian legend could be explained by the fact that my father's best friend was in love with my mother. They formed the same triangle that you have with Arthur, Lancelot, and Guinevere. But it hadn't occurred to me until I had this objectivity, until I became an audience member myself rather than being inside the film.

CLASSICISM VERSUS BRUTALISM

I work in a particular way, which I suppose you could say is quite classical, in the sense, for instance, that I don't move the camera unless there is a purpose for moving it. Also I don't cut unless it's a necessary cut. Which doesn't mean I'm against experimentation—far from it. But for me, it works on a different level. For instance, the most experimental film that I made was probably *Leo the Last,* where I was using a kind of postmodern technique of making the audience aware of the fact that it was a film, that it was a fabrication, that it was artifice. The subject was commenting on the film. That is why it begins with Marcello Mastroianni coming down the street in a car, with a song that says "You look like a movie star." The film was a failure, in the sense that it didn't reach people, which may be the definition of something experimental.

In any case, the grammar I normally use is the one that I learned early on from silent films. If you look at D. W. Griffith's use of close-up and vignetting, for instance, and the way he uses close-ups to illustrate thought, you can see that the modern cinema is often quite crude compared to what was being done then. In terms of visual grammar, for me, the spatial relationship between the characters is the vital thing. If characters are emotionally close, I bring them physically close. If they're emotionally distant, I separate them. That's why I like to use Cinemascope, because it allows you to play with that, to bring space between the actors.*

So, for instance, in *The General*, you'll notice that the robbery sequence, which conventionally today would be done with lots of fast cuts, is done with long takes, and all the action is within the frame. As opposed to what I call "new brutalism" in cinema, which is a form of naïveté, because it's made by people who I think don't really have a grasp of cinema's history. It's the MTV kind of editing, where the main idea is that the more disorienting it is, the more exciting. And you see it creeping into mainstream cinema more and more. You look at something like *Armageddon* and you see all the things that would have been forbidden in classical cinema, like crossing the line, camera jumping from side to side. It is a way to artificially generate excitement, but it doesn't really have any basis to it. And I find it kind of sad, because it's like an old man trying to dress like a teenager.

GIVING LIFE TO A SCENE

My main goal, when I tackle a scene, is obviously to give it as much life as possible. In order to accomplish that, the first thing I do is rehearse. Not on the shooting day itself, but before. And I don't do anything spatial with the actors. It's just a question of exploring the scene. I find that what's really helpful with the actors is to improvise what happens *before* and *after* that scene. Then, when I get on the set for the actual shoot, I start in the morning, work on the first shot, set the camera down, get the composition, and put the marks down for the actors while they're still in make-up.

*Cinemascope is the widest screen format used in cinema, with an aspect ratio of 2.35:1 (meaning that the horizontal part of the frame is 2.35 times longer than the vertical part). Most films have a 1.66:1 or 1.85:1 aspect ratio.

Something I always use to make the compositions is the old Mitchell sidefinder, an instrument that used to be on the side of cameras before they had [through-the-lens] reflex. It's a big thing which you have to hold up in front of you, and instead of putting your eye into something, you step away from it and you can see the composition like a picture, like a frame. Deciding where to set the camera is both a very logical process—where the question of point of view is very important—and an intuitive one.

When film started, of course, the process was much simpler. Cameras were placed like an audience in a theater, and you just had a static shot of the action on stage. So you can imagine what happened when Griffith started moving the camera and the camera became a sort of God's-eye view, an omniscient view that could move anywhere. This gave cinema another dimension altogether. It brought cinema, I think, close to the condition of dreaming. When I spent some time living in the Amazon with a primitive tribe, trying to explain what film was like, and how you could travel from place to place, look at things from different angles, and cut both in space and time, I remember the shaman of the tribe said, "Oh yes, I do that too. When I go into a trance, I travel like that." So I think the power of cinema has to do with the way that it connects to people's dream experiences. Particularly if it's in black and white, because we tend to dream in black and white. So when we set the camera down, I think what we're accomplishing is nothing short of trying to make a dream concrete.

SHOOTING VERSUS EDITING

I don't cover my scenes very much, and I don't like to do a lot of takes, either.* The reason is that, first of all, what I try to do is show the actors that whenever the camera rolls, that's going to be in the movie. If you're shooting from all different angles, then the attitude that prevails is "This probably won't end up ～ in the film, so let's not bother too much." So I try to get a constant tension going. Everything has to be really prepared, and then when the camera's going, that's it. Everybody has to get to a peak of performance at that point. And I never print more than two takes. It's so boring to sit through hours and hours of dailies, and you lose your judgment, eventually. You see six takes, you don't remember what the first one was like. So I shoot very little film. I don't shoot master shots, for instance, and consequently, it's very easy to cut together. I shoot five days instead of six, like most people, and this way I spend at least a day in the cutting room, which is enough to cover one week's worth of shooting. And then I have another day to prepare all the shots for the coming week.

Of course, making the decision to not cover too much means I might get stuck in the editing room and regret it. It's the big dilemma. Kurosawa solved this problem in an interesting way. As he progressed, his films were more and more precisely planned. But when he got to the cutting room, he often regretted not having more material. So he hired a camera operator whose job was to discreetly take shots in every scene, usually with a long lens. He would shoot close-ups when Kurosawa was doing a master shot, he would shoot inserts or cutaways in a dialogue scene, and so on. And then Kurosawa would process that film only if he needed it for cutting. He

---

*Covering a scene means shooting it from different angles, with frames of various sizes, to allow the director more choices when editing.

never asked what had been filmed, because he didn't want the random element to interfere with his planning. I think he was right, because if you shoot with two cameras, which I never do, then you have to make compromises between the two. And filming is all about focusing everything onto a certain point. But if you have two cameras, you're constantly compromising that.

TAILOR THE PART TO THE ACTOR, NOT THE OPPOSITE

Surprisingly, documentaries were probably the best training I got to direct actors. Because what I learned from them, more than anything, was about human behavior. So because I had been observing real people closely, I was able to bring something to actors to help them achieve a feeling of reality. In any case, the key to directing actors is to provide them with a safe environment, a trusting environment, in which they can work. That means giving them structure, making sure they're not distracted by other things that happen on the set. Giving them the focus of your attention, watching them closely, showing them that you're not going to let them make mistakes, that you're not going to put them into difficulty. Then they will be more willing to take chances, which is what you want.

The thing is to listen to actors, because good actors always have important contributions to make. I think an inexperienced director will feel that he will have to go in there and tell the actors what to do. And to be strong and to impose his will. But it's often more important to listen to them, and to make corrections. Then, by the time you get to the set, there's very little to be said, provided you've prepared it right, that you know where you're heading. It's really a matter of making little adjustments. Of course, casting is also essential. Choosing actors is always very painful, because you have an idea of the character in your mind, but you can never find an actor that matches up to that. I feel that each time you cast a part, you're giving part of the film away. But you give the part to an actor, and he comes back to you, and presents you with a performance which usually differs from your preconception. And the answer there, the smart thing to do, is to alter the part to suit the actor, to rewrite it for the actor, rather than to force the actor into the way the part is written.

THE MORE I LEARN, THE LESS I KNOW

Technically speaking, if you compare it to, say, aeronautical engineering, film is quite simple. It's a nineteenth-century invention. You could learn the theory in a few weeks. But then, once you try to put it into practice, you realize you have to deal with so many variables—people, weather, egos, story— there are so many factors that to control them all is impossible. I remember Jean-Luc Godard once told me, "You have to be young and foolish to make a movie. Because if you know as much as we do, it becomes impossible." What he meant was that when you can foresee all the problems, it paralyzes you.

Very often, first films are very good because the director didn't realize how difficult it was going to be. I know that when I started out, I had that reckless foolishness which was very creative. At the same time, I had the fear and terror, each day, that things were going to fall apart. Now, of course, I've become more cautious. But I also don't feel fear anymore, I feel more comfortable on the set, I know it's where I belong. But it doesn't mean I feel I know everything about filmmaking. Quite on the contrary. I spent some time with David Lean just before he died. At the time, he was preparing *Nostromo*, and he said, "I hope I'll be able to make this film, because I feel that I'm just beginning to get the hang of it." I feel very much like that. In fact, I would even say that the more films I make, the less I feel I know.

Films: *Catch Us if You Can (Having a Wild Weekend)* (1965), *Point Blank* (1967), *Hell in the Pacific* (1968), *Leo the Last* (1970), *Deliverance* (1972), *Zardoz* (1974), *The Heretic: Exorcist II* (1977), *Excalibur* (1981), *The Emerald Forest* (1985), *Hope and Glory* (1987), *Where the Heart Is* (1990), *Beyond Rangoon* (1995), *Lumière et compagnie* (1995), *The General* (1999), *The Tailor of Panama* (2001)

SYDNEY POLLACK

b. 1934, Lafayette, Indiana

Here is a man you could listen to for hours. Not just because of what he says, but because he has a totally captivating personality. Sydney Pollack is cerebral but down-to-earth, seasoned but passionate. He has a natural authority but always makes you feel completely at ease. And I can easily understand why other directors sometimes ask him to act in their films, usually with great results.

Pollack is probably the most "Hollywood" of all the directors I've met, in the sense that he only does big studio films, usually with huge budgets and big-name stars. His more recent films, such as Sabrina *or* Random Hearts, *may be a little less edgy than those he made in the seventies, such as* Three Days of the Condor *or* They Shoot Horses, Don't They?, *and perhaps less sweeping than* Out of Africa. *Yet one thing remains absolutely constant in all of them: the quality of acting. Actors who work with Pollack once are usually so happy with the results that they volunteer eagerly for future projects. Most actors who haven't had the opportunity are waiting for their turn. Naturally, I therefore expected that most of our master class would center around directing actors, but, to my delight, Sydney Pollack had much more to say about all the other aspects of making films.*

Master Class with Sydney Pollack

I never chose to make films, really, and, in a way, it is only after I became a director that I started to learn filmmaking. So I
did it backwards, in a way. I had been teaching acting for four
years or so when somebody suggested that I become a director, and before I knew it, I was making films for TV, and then
for the big screen. Given my background, I wasn't drawn to
sweeping, visual films. To me, everything was in the performance, in the acting. The rest was just . . . photography. But
then, over the years, I began to understand filmmaking as a
syntax, as a vocabulary, as a language. And I discovered the
satisfaction that could be drawn from giving the audience the
right sequence of information through the way the shots were
framed, or the way the camera movements were set up.

What I realized, in fact, is that filmmaking is essentially
storytelling. I wouldn't say that I make films to tell stories,
though. Not really. My principal interest is in relationships.
To me, relationships are a metaphor for everything else in life:
politics, morality . . . everything. So basically, I make films to
learn more about relationships. But I don't make films to say
anything, because I wouldn't know what to say. I think there
are basically two kinds of filmmakers: those who know and
understand a truth which they want to communicate to the
world, and those who are not quite sure what the answer to
something is and who make the film as a way to try and find
out. That's what I do.

FINDING THE SPINE

It's important not to intellectualize the filmmaking process
too much. And particularly not during the actual shooting. I
might think a lot about the film before I make it, and certainly
after, but I try not to think too much when I'm actually on the

set. The way I work is that I try to determine as early as possible what the theme of the movie is, what central idea is being expressed through the story. Once I know that, once I have figured out a unifying principle, then any decision I make on the set will be influenced by that and will therefore fall into a certain logic. And to me, the success of a film depends on whether or not the choices you make on the set, as a director, remain true to the original idea.

For instance, *Three Days of the Condor* is a film about trust. Robert Redford plays a character who trusts people too easily and who will learn to be more suspicious. Faye Dunaway, on the other hand, plays a woman who trusts no one, and who, through this dramatic situation, will learn to open up. In *Out of Africa*, the central idea is about possession. It's about England trying to own Africa, and it's about Meryl Streep trying to own Redford. If you take both of these films and analyze them, sequence by sequence, then I should be able to justify every choice I've made, as a filmmaker, in regard to their respective themes.

It's a process I often compare to sculpture: you start with a sort of spine, like a skeleton, and then, little by little, you cover it with clay and give it a shape. Now, it's the spine that holds everything together. Without it, the sculpture would just collapse. But the spine must not be visible or it would ruin everything. And it's the same with a movie. If someone walks out of *Three Days of the Condor* and says, "Oh, it's a film about trust," then I have failed as a filmmaker. The audience must not be conscious of it. Ideally, they will understand it in an abstract way. But what's important is that every aspect of the film be coherent because it is motivated by that theme.

Even the set must reflect the central idea of the film. Which is why I used to love wide screen. Most of my early pictures were shot in wide screen because I feel that it allows you to use the background as a reflection—as a metaphor, I would even say—of what is going on in the foreground. When I made *They Shoot Horses, Don't They?* I insisted that it be shot in wide screen, and nobody understood why, because it takes place almost entirely indoors. But it's a mistake to think that the purpose of wide screen is to shoot big scenery. The real purpose of it is to compose frames that have enormous tension and movement in them, to shoot pictures that need a sense of place. Because even if you frame two people in close-up, you still have space to see the background behind them. If I had shot *Horses* with a flat frame, you would have seen two people dancing and nothing else. You would have lost sense of all the madness around.

Ironically, the first film I did not shoot in wide screen was *Out of Africa*. It may seem odd, because this is certainly a film that demanded as big a frame as possible, but by then, it was the mid-eighties, and I realized that most people were going to see the film on video. I didn't want it to be butchered on the small screen.

I MAKE FILMS TO RAISE QUESTIONS

The only way you can make films for an audience is to make them for yourself. Not out of arrogance, but simply for practical reasons. A film has to be entertaining, that's absolutely true. But how can you know what the audience is going to like? You have to use yourself as a reference. That's what I do. And sometimes I'm wrong. When I made *Havana*, I was wrong, but I would still make it the same way today.

I choose projects that interest me, and I've been lucky enough that most of the time, my films interested the audience too. Had I tried to second-guess what the audience wanted to see, however, I'm sure I would have failed, because it's like trying to solve a very complex mathematical problem.

So I make movies about things that fascinate me—about relationships, mostly, as I said earlier. I try to make films that raise questions more than give answers, films that might not really have a conclusion to them, because I don't like it when one person is right and one person is wrong. I mean, if that's the case, it's not worth making the movie, really.

Most of the films I've made have contained within them an argument regarding the way of life of two people. I have to admit I tend to be slightly more sympathetic toward women than men. I'm not sure why, but in my films, women tend to be a little wiser or to have a more humanistic view of things. That's true in a film like *The Way We Were*. If you look at Barbra Streisand's character in that film, I would say that, although there were many silly things about her, in the long run, she was probably more right than he was. And so most of the work I did on that film, from the minute I started working on it, was to strengthen the man's part, the one played by Redford, because it was initially written with her being a very passionate, committed woman, and he was just a guy who didn't care about anything. It was too easy. It wasn't captivating. For me, the interesting question is, how do you make a decision when both people have a valid point? I have no preconceived ideas. I might have preconceived ideas about certain moral acts, but not when it comes to the relationship between two characters. And the harder it is to determine who is right, the better the film is, I think.

A DIRECTOR EXPERIMENTS ON EACH FILM

There is a grammar of filmmaking, a basic grammar that you depart from. Always. And I think it's important to learn the grammar first. Otherwise, it's like calling yourself an abstract painter because you cannot paint something that is real. It's putting the cart before the horse. You can make your own rules, and you can break all the rules you want—people do it all the time—but I think before you do that, you need to understand the basic grammar. The rules give you a standard, a reference, from which you can then create something original.

For instance, if you want to create tension, or make the audience uncomfortable, you might deliberately go against the rules of composition and make a character look toward the short side of the frame and not the long side. Doing something like that unbalances the picture slightly and might give you the tension you need. But you will get that idea only if you first learn what a balanced frame is.

In any case, I think that there is a degree of experimentation on every film. On *Horses*, for instance, I learned to rollerskate, and I used a skydiving camera mounted on a helmet to film some of the dance sequences because there was no Steadicam at the time, and the machinery was much too heavy to do certain moves.* We had huge dollies that took twenty grips to push just one cameraman on a stool; it was ridiculous. On *Out of Africa*, I was faced with a big lighting problem because I discovered that the light near the equator is very ugly. It's a straight, stripped-down light that has enormous contrast. The tests we did with regular film stock were dreadful to look at. So we decided to experiment, and we went backwards, meaning that we used the fastest film we could find, which was around 3000 ASA. We had to underexpose it considerably, of course, but it was so low-contrast that it gave the film a very soft look. And on the days when it was overcast, we used the slowest film we had and overexposed it

---

*The Steadicam is a device created in the late seventies as a brilliant compromise between hand-held camera moves and dolly moves. Thanks to a complex system of harness, springs, mechanical arm, and video monitor, the Steadicam allows the cameraman to run, jump, climb stairs, and so on—things a bulky dolly cannot do—without the shakiness of regular hand-held camera moves.

two stops, and then printed it down, which gave us a very rich look.*

Another film on which I experimented was *The Firm*. What I decided on this film was that no shot would be still. On every shot of every scene, the cameraman, John Seale, always had his hand on the zoom or on the head of the tripod, and he would move the camera a little bit. It's almost imperceptible, and he did it so slowly that you only notice it if you're looking for it. But I think it helps create the feeling of instability that was necessary to the story. And really, the only reason to experiment must be to serve the story. If you're trying things just because they might look good, I think it's a waste of time.

KEEP ACTORS FROM ACTING

Often, when I read a scene in a script, I get a strange feeling, as if I'm hearing the music of that scene in my head. It's sort of abstract, but when I get on the set, it's that music that really helps me decide where to put the camera. I tend to cover each scene a lot, mostly if they're dialogue scenes, because of matching problems. Sometimes I get a very straightforward scene, where I know there's really only one way to shoot it, and I stick to that. But that's pretty rare.

In any case, I usually start with the actors. And when they get on the set, the first thing I do is send everyone else away. Even a cat or a dog. Actors are very self-conscious. I don't care what they say; I know they can easily be humiliated and that they might not try certain things if people are watching. I never give an actor directions in front of other actors. Because

---

*"Fast" and "slow" refer to the sensitivity of the film stock. The more light available, the lower the film speed needed and the sharper the image will be. Fast film is normally used for low-light conditions but provides poor picture quality. As always with chemical reactions, experimentation can give surprising results, as was the case here.

otherwise, when he does the scene again, he knows that I'm watching and judging him, of course, but he also knows that the other actors are watching and judging him! So it's a very private process. In fact, the first thing I do is keep the actors from acting. I say, "No acting, no performance, just read the lines." That relaxes them a lot.

What I'm trying to do, really, is hold the acting until it happens by itself. Because it will. Pretty soon they'll start moving around as they say their lines, and you'll get a sense of what they want to do. I never tell them, "You go there and you sit here," because then they feel excluded from the process; they feel like they're not a part of it. I might start directing a little bit, but I do it very progressively. My feeling is, if there are seven things wrong with the scene, just talk about one. Then, once it's fixed, talk about another one, and so on. Solve problems one at a time. You can't ask an actor to think about five different things at a time. You have to be patient.

I never spend too much time on rehearsals because I'm always afraid I might get it right in the rehearsals and that it'll be gone in the performance. So once I think we're getting there, I bring the crew in and send the actors to their trailers for make-up and wardrobe, and then I go see each of the actors privately and talk to them some more about the scene. That way, each actor has a different sense of what he or she will bring back to the set. And then, once they get on the set, I always try to roll the camera too soon. It makes the actors a little tense, it catches them off guard a little, and it tends to give better results.

AN ACTOR DOES NOT NEED TO UNDERSTAND

There are lots of truths about directing actors. Some directors understand them intuitively, and some don't. I think the most common mistake a director can make is to direct too much.

When given such huge responsibilities, it's easy to feel like you're not doing your job if you're not constantly telling people what to do. But the truth is, that's silly. If everything is going OK, you should just shut up and be glad. The more you work, the more you realize how little this job requires. Well, it does require a lot, but there is a much simpler, a more economical, and, ultimately, a more efficient way to do it than to always be telling people what to do.

The other important thing to know, I think, is that acting has nothing to do with intellectuality. An actor doesn't need to understand in a conventional way what he is doing—he just has to do it. And so you have to make a distinction between direction that produces behavior and direction that produces intellectual understanding, the latter being absolutely useless. Most young directors will talk for hours about the meaning of a scene and never direct behavior. That won't make the actor angrier or more touching in the scene. He only needs to understand what he needs to live truthfully in an imaginary set of circumstances. Because all acting comes from wanting something. It's what you want that makes you do something, not what you think.

THE REAL CHALLENGE IS THE STORY

When I did some work for the Sundance Institute, all the young directors I met were frightened of actors. They were terrified at the idea of having to direct actors. So the advice I gave them, which I would give to any beginning filmmaker, is that they should go and observe an acting class. Better yet, they should take a class and learn a little bit about acting because that's the best way to understand what an actor does—and does not—need in order to function.

The other thing I would say to a beginning filmmaker is that technique is something to fall back on when things don't happen by themselves. If things do happen by themselves, accept your good luck with gratitude and keep quiet. If you know that you have a great script, that you cast your film right, and that you have a great cinematographer, and if when you start rehearsing on the set things work out fine, then keep quiet. Don't mess it up. Learning to keep quiet is as important as learning what to say.

Of course, I understand that there might be a desire for challenge. But then make the story the challenge, not the technique. When I started working on *Three Days of the Condor*, for instance, I was only interested in the romance between Robert Redford and Faye Dunaway. The rest was just background to me. And the challenge in that story was to make the audience believe that a man and a woman meeting in such dramatic circumstances (he has kidnapped her) could end up falling in love in less than two days. I call that a *"Richard III* challenge" because of the scene in the Shakespeare play where a man actually seduces the widow of his dead enemy just hours after he's killed him. I think it's amazing to be able to accomplish something like that. Of course, it's not easy, and you have more chances to fail than to succeed. But if you play it safe, I can assure you that you will never achieve anything interesting.

Films: *The Slender Thread* (1965), *This Property Is Condemned* (1966), *The Scalphunters* (1968), *Castle Keep* (1969), *They Shoot Horses, Don't They?* (1969), *Jeremiah Johnson* (1972), *The Way We Were* (1973), *The Yakuza* (1975), *Three Days of the Condor* (1975), *Bobby Deerfield* (1977), *The Electric Horseman* (1979), *Absence of Malice* (1981), *Tootsie* (1982), *Out of Africa* (1985), *Havana* (1990), *The Firm* (1993), *Sabrina* (1995), *Random Hearts* (1999)

CLAUDE SAUTET

b. 1924, Montrouge, France; d. 2000, Paris, France

There are directors who are able to capture in an authentic and visceral way the essence of the times they live in, as though they have their finger on the pulse of a whole nation. So it was with Claude Sautet in the seventies. When The Things of Life (Les choses de la vie) *came out, it was as if an entire generation of middle-class Frenchmen in their forties were handed a mirror in which they could look at all their flaws and weaknesses. And they loved it. Then times changed. In the much less political and introspective eighties, people started to turn away from Claude Sautet's films. For my generation, his films were those our parents loved, so they were automatically rejected. In addition, Sautet himself seemed less inspired in that period. It was only in the nineties that he came back with two very powerful films,* A Heart in Winter *and* Nelly and Monsieur Arnaud, *which reminded everybody what a fantastic filmmaker he was.*

Today French people will often say "a Claude Sautet–type film" when trying to talk about a style that depicts life in a natural and humane way. That, I think, is the greatest reward he could hope for. I met with Sautet two years after he'd directed the hugely successful Nelly and Monsieur Arnaud. *Everybody was eagerly awaiting his next film, but, sadly, Sautet died of cancer the following year. Journalists who knew him said he was not only a great interviewee but a great person to get to know. They were right. Shy yet incredibly direct, Claude Sautet chained-smoked all day. He was hypersensitive and somewhat clumsy, but he was a man you couldn't help but like. I know many in France—and film fans all over the world—miss him today.*

▨ Master Class with Claude Sautet

It was more through chance than anything else that I got into filmmaking. But what I found there was something I didn't expect: a means of communicating certain emotions that words couldn't easily define, and which, up until that point, I thought only music could reveal in a nonexplicative manner.

I should point out that I started reading at a fairly late age, around sixteen, and because of this I suffered for many years from a lack of vocabulary and some difficulty in expressing my thoughts. Ideas would come together in my mind in a rather abstract manner, with a structure that was more like music. I had no musical talent, but I discovered that film, in fact, offered just about the same structure and the same potential for expression. In jazz, for instance, there's a theme, and once this theme has been established, each player is free to improvise on it. It's the same thing with film: there's a horizontal axis (the theme and the story) that remains constant and a vertical axis (the tone) that each director develops in his own way. The only difference is that film is a recorded image which possesses an inescapable documentary power. In other words, a film is a dream, but it's a dream made up of reality. Therefore, you need to retain a certain rigor in the freedom that you take. You can do a great deal with film, but you can't do everything.

A FILM IS ABOVE ALL AN ATMOSPHERE

I don't think any self-respecting filmmaker can be content with directing only. And even if they're not officially credited with the screenplay, most serious directors "steer" the writing of their films. If they leave the task of writing to others, that's because the concentration required to correctly write a screenplay takes up a huge amount of energy, and directors prefer to keep this energy to focus on directing. Personally, one of the reasons why I don't work alone on screenplays is that it bores me and I quickly lose heart. But, above all, I don't work alone because I need another person's vision. I need to discuss things that are confused and contradictory within me. When I start writing a film, I don't have a story. It's more abstract than that. I usually just have ideas about characters and relationships.

You have to understand that the films that made me want to direct are the American B movies of the forties and fifties. What I liked about them was their total lack of literary pretension. The directors simply filmed the actions of their characters with enough attention and compassion to bring them to life. As a result, of course, a large part of their personality was left in the dark. That's what I liked, and I've always attempted to re-create that in my films. It's what I call "a portrait in motion"—in other words, a sort of snapshot that, unavoidably, always remains incomplete or unfinished.

This is why I never start out with a story but with something more abstract that you could call the atmosphere. In fact, everything begins with a jumbled obsession that I find hard to explain and that I try to sum up by imagining characters, by creating a relationship between them, and by trying to find the most intense point in this relationship—in other words, the moment of crisis. Once I have that, I have my theme. Then my work consists of exposing this theme through film techniques, delaying it, speeding it up, or hurling it forward, often by indirect means. And that's how the climate is created.

Directors who manage to summarize their films always impress me. For example, if someone were to ask me what *The Things of Life* is about, I wouldn't know how to reply other than to say, "It's about a guy who has a car accident." Otherwise, I would go into endless detail.

FILMING THE UNSPOKEN

If you were to ask thirty directors to shoot the same scene, you'd probably discover thirty different approaches. One of them would shoot everything in a single take; another would use a series of brief shots; and yet another would use only close-ups, focusing on faces and so forth. It's all a matter of point of view. There's no hard-and-fast rule—there can't really be one because directing is wholly dependent on the physical relationship between a filmmaker and the set that is being filmed. You can read the screenplay and think, "I know, I'll start this scene with a close-up." But it isn't until you're on the set and the actors have taken over their characters that the process of filming becomes material.

Personally—and I like speaking about this because people have often reproached me about it—I always try to film as simply as possible. I almost always film a conversation with reverse-angle shots.* People tell me that the reverse-angle is a TV technique. Maybe, but on TV, it's a TV reverse-angle. In film, it's very different. On TV, it's a method that allows you to save time. In film, on the contrary, I make the most of this simplicity to try out all kinds of things: I change lenses from one shot to the next, change rhythm, change the size of the frame, film over the shoulder or avoid doing so, place mirrors behind the actors, and so on. Often, I even oblige the actor who is off-frame to speak the lines differently, or I speak them myself, to create an element of surprise and unease in the actor being filmed. I like to create uncertainty between the characters because this helps give them greater presence. Above all, on TV, people are worried about moments of silence. In film, it's the opposite: stares and silence are an integral part of

---

*A reverse-angle shot is the most basic way to shoot a conversation, in which the camera goes back and forth between two medium shots of two people talking to each other.

the plot. And from that point of view, a simple reverse-angle shot can easily become a confrontation. I feel that these scenes aren't there to get information across through the dialogue but, on the contrary, to express what is going on behind the words and what is generally left unsaid.

I have taken this idea very far at times. I remember, for instance, that when I finished cutting *Mado*, I realized the lead actor hardly says anything for the first half of the film. I thought, "Damn, he doesn't speak, that's a problem." But, in fact, he didn't need to speak. Anything he could have said would simply have harmed the character. In any case, I realize that most of the time, dialogue is an appalling succession of clichés. The only thing that makes any difference is the intonation. The same words spoken with different tones can alter the whole dramatic intensity of a scene. And this is all the more striking when you see your film dubbed into another language, say, German or Italian. The intonation is no longer the same, and, all of a sudden, it's as if the actors themselves had changed faces.

EVERYTHING IS BASED ON INSTINCT

Whatever your level of preparation for a film, reality will inevitably oblige you to improvise most of your decisions on the set. The human factor is obviously one of the most unpredictable elements, the one that most frequently obliges you to question things.

On *The Things of Life*, for instance, at the start of shooting, I discovered that one of the actors froze as soon as the camera was too close to him. He simply couldn't perform. I realized that the only way to get anything out of him was to move the camera back and to film him with a very long lens. In fact, it helped him give a better performance. But, as a result, it forced me to change the film's whole visual style, since I couldn't film the other actors with different lenses. That wouldn't have been consistent. So you see, sometimes a very minor detail can influence a whole film.

But the element that has the greatest impact on the director's work—and it would be absurd to claim otherwise—is the economic factor. The more "realistic" approach of French New Wave cinema, for instance, was closely linked to questions of budget.* At the time, people felt that shooting in natural settings was cheaper. Therefore, they would shoot in real apartments rather than in film studios. But such decisions necessarily have important consequences for the film's aesthetic characteristics. When you shoot in a studio, you try to bring an artificial setting to life, whereas in the opposite case, you attempt to stylize an overly realistic set. Therefore, in the studio, the stylistic approach consists of creating disorder, and on location, it consists of creating order. That changes a great number of things. In addition, in a natural setting you're forced to use lenses with short focal lengths and to limit the camera movements because you can't move the walls out of the way as you can in a studio. All this ends up having its influence on the film's visual aspect.

Today, people have realized that shooting on location can often be more costly than shooting in the studio because you need to close off streets, park trucks, bring in generators, and so on. So they're returning to the studio, toward a more traditional aesthetic form. You gain in comfort, but you lose what only shooting on location can bring you—that is, the unforeseen elements that are often a source of original ideas. When confronted with all these exterior elements, the only way to

*"New Wave" is the name given to the group of French filmmakers who, in the sixties, transformed cinema by bringing it out of the studios and into the streets, for economic, artistic, and political reasons. They stripped their films of all the "artificial" and glamorous aspects of cinema and showed the audience that real life could be as fascinating as fantasy. They are the original impulse behind everything that might be called "realistic" in cinema today.

make decisions is to rely on your instinct and focus on the abstract idea that has been guiding you since the writing of the screenplay and on which you must remain steadfast until the end of shooting. You must remain faithful to your instinct because in the end, your instinct is the only thing that justifies making one decision rather than another.

KEEP YOUR DISTANCE, BUT STAY CLOSE

When it comes to breaking down a scene, there's never any obvious way to do it. There are only problems for which you try to find the best solution possible. I know, for example, that I am incapable of shooting what people call an establishing shot—a fairly wide shot at the start of a scene that shows the audience where we are. I've tried, but I can never pull it off. I don't know why. So, each time I start a scene in a new setting, I try to break it down in such a way that the audience will discover the setting without realizing it, through the characters' actions.

This is why I always begin by working with the actors on the set. I act as if they were free to place themselves wherever they choose, but they don't really know where to position themselves. So I suggest a few things. I tell them, "You can stay sitting there or start here and move from there to there." We do that until they feel that the movements are natural, rehearsing the dialogue very little. They simply speak their lines quietly, just to check that everything works. Then I talk with the director of photography and we try to find the best angles to shoot the movements that have been worked out.

The whole problem of directing, at this point, is to find out how to be both close and distant, how to be inside the character while keeping a strategic distance. It's a process that requires a great deal of concentration. When the director of photography suggests a frame, I take a look and then accept or refuse it. But while we're shooting, I never check the monitor, first because I prefer to look at the actors directly—and I think that they too prefer that—and second because I like the idea of the DP being the film's first audience in a way, through the lens. I think it's important to delegate this kind of responsibility because it makes people put more into their work. Obviously, there are times when I view the dailies and realize that the camera operator hasn't at all filmed what we planned and that we'll need to reshoot it. That's never very pleasant, of course. But it's part of the game.

EVERY ACTOR WANTS TO PERFORM

The very basis for directing actors is trust. Given the kind of films that I make, it's very important for me to find actors who have sufficient confidence—in themselves and in me—to reveal their most vulnerable side. Several times, actors have said to me, "I don't have any lines in this scene. Isn't that a problem? If I don't say anything, won't people get the impression that I'm not thinking anything?" So I reassure them and explain what Anglo-Saxon countries understood a long time ago, namely, that the actor who stares has more presence than the actor who speaks.

Everything depends, of course, on the way the actor stares. There are actors who are worried about their ability to express something when there are no verbal indications, and you need to give them confidence in their bare existence. Similarly, some actresses don't want to have their hair pulled back because they feel naked. It's what I prefer because they have no possibility for concealment and so perform better.

This is something that I discovered with Romy Schneider, of course. During the rehearsals for *The Things of Life*, I saw her once with her hair up and I thought, "What a difference, it's incredible—she doesn't even need to speak!" Since then, I have often used this with actresses because they give off more power and sensitivity this way.

But before you can direct an actor well, you need to *choose* the right actor. And that requires a fair number of meetings, conversations in which you talk about everything: politics, childhood, troubled moments . . . After a while, a climate of trust is created, and, indirectly, you discover a great deal about the potential of the actor, who can't control his image at that point because he isn't being filmed. He ends up revealing aspects of his personality, and you need to reward him for showing his vulnerability by making him understand that this is what interests you. The rest—in other words, knowing whether the actor corresponds to the part—is much less important than people think, for the simple reason that every actor wants to perform and, if possible, to perform as someone who isn't like him or her at all. So the real problem isn't knowing whether the actor matches the character but whether he or she matches me. Moreover, actors know this. When I met Michel Serrault for *Nelly and Monsieur Arnaud*, he had just read the screenplay and I asked him if he was interested in the part. He smiled and immediately replied, "What about me? Do I interest you?" It's all a matter of personality. You can get an actor to read clichés, but if his personality is powerful enough, there won't be any clichés.

WHAT OUR FILMS TEACH US

I've never been truly satisfied with any of my films. Generally, at the end of editing, I tell myself that I didn't do too badly after all. Often the film is not exactly what I wanted to make, but it's close. However, when I see the film again a few years later, I'm usually dismayed. I see things that seem terribly awkward and clumsy to me. True, there are other things that I find fairly beautiful and that even have a certain grace, but since I am generally incapable of understanding or remembering how I obtained them, this is almost even more depressing!

Seeing your films later is always an instructive experience. You usually discover that, out of concern for clarity, you stressed some things when, in fact, they were totally explicit. That's one of the great lessons you learn from your first films. You realize that the cinematic language offers all kinds of tricks to explain without explaining.

Seeing your films again, you also discover all the things that they have in common, all the things that you systematically put into them without being aware of it. Personally, with hindsight, I can clearly perceive my mania of always tackling male characters more critically than female ones, which probably comes from my childhood and the fact that I grew up with an absent father. All kinds of things like that return in each film, whether I want them to or not. The sets change, the characters too, but the same underlying themes return. In fact, despite all the energy that I've put into each new project to make it different, in the end I've been making the same film all my life.

Films: *Bonjour sourire* (unreleased in the U.S.) (1955), *The Big Risk* (*Classe tous risques*) (1960), *The Dictator's Guns* (*L'arme à gauche*) (1965), *The Things of Life* (*Les choses de la vie*) (1970), *Max* (*Max et les ferrailleurs*) (1971), *César and Rosalie* (*César et Rosalie*) (1972), *Vincent, François, Paul . . . and the Others* (*Vincent, François, Paul . . . et les autres*) (1974), *Mado* (1976), *A Simple Story* (*Une histoire simple*) (1978), *Un mauvais fils* (unreleased in the U.S.) (1980), *Waiter!* (*Garçon!*) (1983), *A Few Days with Me* (*Quelques jours avec moi*) (1988), *A Heart in Winter* (*Un cœur en hiver*) (1992), *Nelly and Monsieur Arnaud* (*Nelly et Monsieur Arnaud*) (1995)

REVISIONISTS

Woody Allen
Bernardo Bertolucci
Martin Scorsese
Wim Wenders

There seems to be a consensus among film aficionados that the decade of the seventies was the most prolific and innovative that cinema has ever known. These four filmmakers were fortunate enough to begin their careers during that time, when they were free—even encouraged—to reinvent the rules of cinema, in terms of both form and content, and to use film in any number of ways: as a tool of political expression, as a means of personal introspection, as a merciless mirror aimed at society, or as a medium through which to explore new forms of storytelling.

WOODY ALLEN

b. 1935, Brooklyn, New York

French film buffs have always regarded Woody Allen as a near deity. In his facetious way, the director attributes his enthusiastic following in France to "clever subtitling." Yet few filmmakers have produced such a large and diverse body of personal work (thirty-five films in thirty-five years). Allen is an artist in the truest sense, and that may be why he has remained somewhat secluded from the rest of the film world, residing on that island between Europe and America called Manhattan. For years, my chances of interviewing him were as slim as chatting with the Abominable Snowman in the Himalayas. Then, in the late nineties, for some reason, Allen's attitude toward publicity changed radically. I was one of the first journalists in Paris to have the pleasure of talking to him one-on-one. At the time I met him in 1996 for this master class, he had just directed Everybody Says I Love You, *a film of his that, for the first time in many years, had been as well received in the United States as in France.*

Allen is just as fascinating, articulate, and witty in person as he is in his films. I was nervous at first because his publicists had granted me very little time for the interview. However, Allen proceeded calmly, never hesitated, never went off track, and never left a sentence unfinished. The whole interview was done in half an hour, and the text that follows is an almost exact transcription of our conversation.

▇ Master Class with Woody Allen

I've never been asked to teach filmmaking, and, frankly, I've never been tempted, either. Well, actually, Spike Lee, who teaches a class at Harvard, once asked me to talk to his students. I was perfectly happy to do it, but in the end, it was a little bit frustrating. The problem is, I feel there's so little you can teach, really, and I didn't want to be discouraging to them. Because the truth of the matter is, you either have it or you don't. If you don't have it, you can study all your life and it won't mean anything. You won't become a better filmmaker for it. And if you do have it, then you will quickly learn to use the few tools you need. Most of what you need, as a director, is psychological help, anyhow. Balance, discipline, things like that. The technical aspect comes second. Many talented artists are destroyed by their neuroses, their doubts, and their angst, or they let too many exterior things distract them. That's where the danger lies, and these are the elements that a writer or filmmaker should try to master first.

So, to come back to Spike Lee's class, there wasn't a lot I could teach, really. The students would ask me things such as "How did you know, in *Annie Hall*, that you could just stop the film and talk directly to the audience?" And all I could answer to them was "Well, it was my instinct to do it this way." And that, I think, is the most important lesson I've learned about filmmaking: that for those who can do it, there's no big mystery to it. One should not be intimidated by it or get caught up in thinking it's some kind of mysterious, complex thing to do. Just follow your instinct. And if you have talent, it won't be hard. And if you don't, then it will be impossible.

DIRECTORS MAKE FILMS FOR THEMSELVES

First of all, I think there are two distinct kinds of directors: those who write their own material and those who don't. It is very rare that you can be both and alternate between films you write and films you don't. Now, I don't mean that one of these two categories is better than the other, or that one type of director is more admirable than the other. They're just different. The one thing you get when you write your own script is a sort of very idiosyncratic movie all the time. There's a style that emerges very quickly, and certain concerns tend to re-appear more often. So with that kind of director, the audience is more in contact with a personality. Whereas if a director adapts a different writer's script every time, he might do a brilliant job on it and—if the script is good—it might turn out to be a truly great film, but you'll never have that personal quality that an author has. Now, this can be for better or for worse: you can write your own script and have a film with a personal quality, but if you have nothing interesting or new to say about life, then your films will never be as good as those of a director who adapts a good script.

Once this distinction is made, I think that all directors should make their films for themselves, and that their duty is to make sure that, whatever obstacles they might have to face, the film is—and remains—theirs from beginning to end. The director must remain the master of the film, always. As soon as he has become the slave, he has lost. Now, when I say you have to make the film for yourself, I don't mean that you should do it with contempt toward the audience. But my own personal feeling is that if you make a film that pleases you, and you make it well, then you will please the audience too, or at least part of the audience. But I think it's a mistake to try to guess what the audience will like and try to do that. Because then you might as well just let the audience come onto the set and direct the film for you.

WHEN I GET ON THE SET, I DON'T KNOW ANYTHING

Every director has his own way of working. I know many of them arrive on the set in the morning knowing exactly what they're going to shoot, and how. Two weeks before being on the set, they know. They know the lens they're going to use, the way they're going to frame, how many shots they will do . . . I'm the opposite of that. When I get on the set, I have absolutely no idea how I'm going to shoot what I have to shoot—and I haven't tried to think about it, either. I like to arrive with no preconceived idea. I never rehearse; I never visit the set before I'm going to shoot. I get there in the morning, and depending on how I feel that morning, and what comes over me at that moment, I decide what I'm going to do. I admit it, it's not a great way to work. It's comfortable for me, but most directors I know have always been more prepared.

Also, when it comes to actually shooting, I tend to have, once again, a different approach from other filmmakers. Usually, the director brings the actors onto the set, asks them to play out the scene, and then watches and, according to what's going on, decides with the director of photography where the camera should be set and how many shots are needed. I don't do it that way. What I do is I walk around with the cameraman and see where I want the action to take place and how I want it to look, and then when the actors come in, I ask them to accommodate what I've decided for the camera. I tell them things like, "You say this here, then move over there and say that. You can stay there for a while, but then I want you to move over there to say this." It's a kind of directing that, in a way, resembles theater, and the frame I've chosen defines the borders of the stage, if you will.

But the thing is, I don't do any coverage, and I try to shoot every scene in a single shot, or as close to that as I can. I don't cut as long as I don't have to, and I never shoot the same scene from a different angle. Also, when I cut, I continue the following shot from the exact moment when I cut the last. I never cover anything, partly because I'm too lazy, and partly because I don't like the actors to do the same thing over and over. This way, they can stay fresh and spontaneous, and they can also try lots of different things. They can play the same scene differently every time, without having to worry about whether it'll match with the other shots.

COMEDY REQUIRES SPARTAN DIRECTION

Comedy is a particular genre in that it is very demanding and very strict in terms of directing. The problem here is that nothing can ever get in the way of the laugh. Nothing can ever distract the audience from what is supposed to make them laugh. If you move the camera too much, if you edit too quickly, there's always the risk that you'll kill the laugh. So it's hard to make a fantasy-looking comedy. Comedy has to be real, simple, and clear. You hardly ever get a chance to shoot anything very dramatically. What you want, really, is a nice, clean, open frame, like you have in the Chaplin or Keaton movies. You want to see everything, you want to see the actors do what they do. And you don't want to do anything that will ruin the timing, as timing is everything in comedy. So there's something very spartan about it, which, of course, is quite frustrating for a director. At least, it is for me. And a lot of the more "serious" films I've made were probably a way to get rid of this frustration. Because you always have that filmmaking instinct to step out and try certain things and enjoy the camera and enjoy the movement. But you have to repress that in comedy.

Of course, each director finds a way to work a little bit around the rules. For instance, as I don't like cutting when I do a scene, I use the zoom lens a lot. This way, as I'm shooting, I can zoom on a face to get a close-up, go back to a wide shot, then move into a medium shot. This technique allows me to edit on the set rather than in the editing room. I guess I could get the same result by dollying in and out, which I sometimes do. But there is a slight difference. First of all, there's not always enough room. Then, well, zooming has a rather "functional" aspect, whereas as soon as you actually move the camera, it gives the shot an added emotional impact, which is not always what you want. Sometimes, all you want is to get closer to something to show it better, that's all. You don't necessarily want to show it and shout, "Look! Look!" which camera moves tend to do.

RULES ARE MADE TO BE BROKEN

As important as it is to know how strict the rules of directing comedy are, I think it is also necessary, even vital, to always experiment. Before I did *Zelig*, for instance, I never would have believed it was possible to create a character without ever showing anything more than brief pictures of him getting into a car or walking out of a building. I never would have imagined it was possible to use the documentary format to make a film that was very character-driven and very personal. And yet it worked. I'm not saying you have to go out on a limb like that every time, and I'm not saying this could work every time, but knowing that it's possible is rather reassuring.

Also, if you take *Husbands and Wives*, the way it's shot goes completely against what I said earlier about comedy's visual style. Many people criticized me for the way this film was shot, actually, with the camera on the shoulder and constantly moving. They said it was excessive. But I really feel it's the film in which I've used camera moves in the best way—or, at least, in the most appropriate way. Most directors see camera movements as something you do for pure cinematic pleasure: it's kind of an instrument that you can use to make things more beautiful, and that you have to use with parsimony because you don't want to waste its effect.

Personally, it took me a long time before I started to move the camera. At first because I was inexperienced, and then because I started working with Gordon Willis, a magnificent cinematographer whose peculiarity is that the way he lights a scene usually prevents you from moving around it. Since I started working with Carlo Di Palma, I started using camera moves. It came little by little and then reached its highest possible point on *Husbands and Wives*. And what I like in this film is that for once, the camera moves are not motivated by the sole filmmaking pleasure of the director, but by the story. They reflect the chaotic mental state of the characters; I would even say that they are part of these characters.

TO DIRECT ACTORS, JUST LET THEM DO THEIR WORK

People often ask me what is the secret of directing actors, and they always think I'm being facetious when I answer that all you have to do is hire talented people and let them do their work. But it's true. A lot of directors tend to overdirect their actors, and the actors indulge in that because, well, they like being overdirected. They like having endless discussions about the part; they like to intellectualize the whole process of creating a character. And often, that's how they get confused and lose their spontaneity or their natural talent. Now, I think I know where this all comes from. I think the actors—and probably the director too—feel guilty about doing something that is so easy and so natural to them, and so they try to make it more complex to justify being paid for it. I stay away from that thought process.

Of course, if the actors have a question or two, I answer it as well as I can, but otherwise, I hire talented people and let them do what they're good at. I never force them into anything, I completely trust their acting instinct, and I'm hardly ever disappointed. Also, as I said earlier, I shoot long, uncut scenes, which actors love because that's what acting is all about. Most of the time, in films, they do a three-second shot where they move their head and say two words, and then they have to wait four hours to shoot the end of that scene from another angle. They're just getting warm and then they have to stop. It's extremely frustrating, and I think it goes against the very thing that makes their job enjoyable. So, in any case, whenever one of my films comes out, people are always amazed by how brilliant the acting is—the actors themselves are amazed at how brilliant their acting is, and they treat me like a hero! But the fact is, they're the ones who have done all the work.

A FEW MISTAKES TO AVOID

There are many errors a director must always try to avoid, of course. The first one that comes to my mind is probably to avoid doing anything that doesn't contribute to your vision. It often happens, in the middle of making a film, that you will have a clever idea, or something that you want to try out. But if this idea doesn't belong in your film, then you must have the honesty, or the integrity, to put it aside. Which doesn't mean you have to be rigid or stubborn. On the contrary: this also would be a mistake. A film is like a plant. Once you sow the seeds, it starts to grow organically. And the director must grow at the same rate if he wants to see it to its end. He must be ready to take all sorts of changes into consideration. He must also be open to other people's points of view. When you write, you're alone in a room with a piece of paper: you can control everything. Once on the set, it's a different story. You're still in control, but you need the help of other people to achieve this. This is something you must understand, accept, and appreciate. And you have to work with what you have. Determination is a quality, but intransigence is definitely a mistake.

I also think it's a grave error to start shooting a film with a script that is weak or not ready and to think, "It's OK, I'll fix it on the set." Experience has shown me that if you have a good script, you can do a miserable job of directing and still get a pretty good movie, whereas if you have a bad script, you can do a brilliant job of directing and it will hardly make a difference.

And finally, the biggest danger I would warn any future filmmaker about is to think that you know everything about cinema. I make films today and I'm still surprised—even shocked, sometimes—at the way the audience responds. I think they're going to like this character, and it turns out they're totally indifferent to him, but they like another character whom I had barely thought about. I think they're going to laugh at a certain place, and they end up laughing at something I never thought was so funny. In a way, it's a little frustrating. But that's also what makes this job so magical, so fascinating, and so enjoyable. If I thought I knew everything about it, I would have stopped a long time ago.

Films: *What's Up, Tiger Lily?* (1966), *Take the Money and Run* (1969), *Bananas* (1971), *Everything You Always Wanted to Know About Sex (But Were Afraid to Ask)* (1972), *Sleeper* (1973), *Love and Death* (1975), *Annie Hall* (1977), *Interiors* (1978), *Manhattan* (1979), *Stardust Memories* (1980), *A Mid-*

summer Night's Sex Comedy (1982), *Zelig* (1983), *Broadway Danny Rose* (1983), *The Purple Rose of Cairo* (1985), *Hannah and Her Sisters* (1986), *Radio Days* (1987), *September* (1987), *Another Woman* (1988), *New York Stories* (1989), *Crimes and Misdemeanors* (1989), *Alice* (1990), *Shadows and Fog* (1992), *Husbands and Wives* (1992), *Manhattan Murder Mystery* (1993), *Bullets over Broadway* (1994), *Mighty Aphrodite* (1995), *Everyone Says I Love You* (1996), *Deconstructing Harry* (1997), *Celebrity* (1998), *Sweet and Lowdown* (1999), *Small Time Crooks* (2000), *The Curse of the Jade Scorpion* (2001)

BERNARDO BERTOLUCCI
b. 1941, Parma, Italy

"Serenity" is the first word that comes to mind when I try to describe Bernardo Bertolucci. Sure, he had his wild, rebellious times in the seventies, when he was making provocative and politically oriented films. But as I sat listening to him twenty years later, I couldn't help thinking there was a reason he had recently chosen to make a film about the Buddha. True, there is still a malicious little twinkle in his eye, and I assume he must lose his temper sometimes, but there was nothing but peacefulness radiating from him the day we met at the Locarno Film Festival in Switzerland. He was being honored with a lifetime achievement award in recognition of his impressive career. "I hope this award does not imply that my career is over," he quipped.

People usually remember Bernardo Bertolucci for Last Tango in Paris and The Last Emperor (for which he received nine Oscars). But I consider The Conformist his greatest achievement. The film contains all the elements that make Bertolucci's work so powerful: a political viewpoint, a historical perspective, individual human tragedy, fantastic acting, and probably the best lighting work from one the industry's most inspired directors of photography, Vittorio Storaro (who has worked on nearly all of Bertolucci's films). Bertolucci smiled a little at the idea of giving a master class, surely because he had rejected his own cinema teachers back in the sixties, but he played along gracefully and turned out to have much more to say than he claimed he would.

▪ Master Class with Bernardo Bertolucci

I didn't go to film school. I was lucky enough to work in my youth as an assistant on Pier Paolo Pasolini's films, and that's how I learned about directing. For years, I was proud of this lack of theoretical training, and I still believe that the best possible school is the film set. Then again, I realize that not everyone has this opportunity. And there's another point: in my opinion, to learn to make films, you not only need to make films but also to see as many as possible. These two considerations are of equal importance. And this is probably the only reason I would advise someone to attend film school today: it's an opportunity to discover all kinds of films that you'll never be able to see in theaters.

But if someone were to ask me to teach directing, frankly, I'd be at a loss. I don't think I'd know where to begin. I'd perhaps simply be content with showing films. And the one that I would choose over any other is most certainly *The Rules of the Game* (*La règle du jeu*) by Jean Renoir. I would show students how, in this film, Renoir manages to build a bridge between Impressionism, his father's art, and cinema, his own art. I would try to prove how this film attains the goal that every film should strive for: transporting us to a different place.

LEAVE THE DOOR OPEN

I had the opportunity to meet Jean Renoir in Los Angeles in the seventies. He was almost eighty years old and used a wheelchair. We chatted for an hour, and I was amazed to find that his ideas regarding the cinema were the very same ones that we thought we had discovered with the New Wave, except that he had had them thirty years earlier! At one point, he said something that struck me as the greatest lesson about filmmaking that I have ever learned. He said to me, "You must always leave the door of the set open because you never know what might come in." What he meant by that, of course, is that you must know how to make room for the unforeseen, the unexpected, and the spontaneous since they often create the magic of the cinema.

In my films, I always leave the door open to allow life to enter the set. And, paradoxically, this is why I work with increasingly structured screenplays. If I have a strong situation to work from, I feel more comfortable about improvising. For me, the interest of the unexpected is its appearance in a situation where, in theory, everything is planned out. For instance, if I shoot an exterior scene in full sunlight and clouds drift across the sun in the middle of a take and the light starts to change unexpectedly, I'm in heaven! Especially if the take lasts long enough for the clouds to move on and the sun to come back . . . Things like that are wonderful because they represent the ultimate degree of improvisation.

But "leaving the door open" doesn't concern only elements outside the set. I had written poetry before starting to make films, so at first I looked on the camera as another kind of pen than the one used to write poems. In my mind, I made a film alone; I was its auteur in the strictest sense. Then, with time, I realized that a director can express his fantasies even better if he is able stimulate the creativity of everyone around him. A film is a sort of melting pot in which the talents of a crew must mingle. Film stock is much more sensitive than people think, and it records not only what is in front of the camera but everything around it.

I TRY TO DREAM MY SHOTS

Since I didn't learn directing in a theoretical manner, the notion of film "grammar" doesn't mean anything to me. Moreover, to my way of thinking, if such grammar does exist, it is there to be defied. That is how the cinematic language evolves. When Godard shot *Breathless*, his grammar was "Power to the jump cut."* And the amazing thing is that if you take a look at one of John Ford's last films, *Seven Women*, you see that the director—one of the most traditional in Hollywood—must have seen *Breathless* and started using the jump cut himself, something inconceivable ten years earlier.

For a long time, I tackled each shot as if it were the last, as if someone would be taking my camera away just after I finished shooting with it. Therefore, I had the feeling that I was stealing each shot, and in this state of mind it's impossible to think in terms of "grammar" or even "logic." Even today, I prepare nothing in advance. In fact, I try to dream in my sleep the shots that I will be shooting the next day on the set. With a little luck, I'm able to do it. If not, when I arrive on set in the morning I ask to be alone for a while, and I roam around the set with my viewfinder. I look through it and try to imagine the characters moving and saying their lines. It's almost as if the scene were already there, invisible or impalpable, with me trying to seek it out or give it life. After that, I bring the camera in, I call the actors, and I try to see if what I have imagined works in reality. The rest is a long process of fine-tuning between the camera, the actors, and the light. Therefore, it's a sort of perpetual process in which I try to make sure that each shot gives rise to the next.

---

*The jump cut goes against all the rules of traditional editing (which say that cuts between shots should be smooth and invisible). When handled correctly—as Godard certainly did in *Breathless*, for instance—the jump-cut technique can create wonderful dynamics. When handled badly, it makes the audience think the director does not know what he is doing.

COMMUNICATION OCCURS BEFORE THE FILM

Communication is a vital factor in the smooth running of a film set. This communication must be established prior to filming because it will be almost too late on the set.

For example, when I decided to make *Last Tango in Paris*, I took Vittorio Storaro to see a Francis Bacon exhibit at the Grand Palais in Paris. I showed him the paintings, explaining that this was the kind of thing I wanted to use as my inspiration. And if you look at the finished film, there are orange hues in it that are directly influenced by Bacon. Then I took Marlon Brando to see the same exhibit, and I showed him the painting that you see at the start of the film during the titles. It's a portrait that seems fairly figurative when you first see it. But when you look at it for some time, it loses its naturalism completely and becomes the expression of what is happening in the painter's subconscious. I said to Marlon, "You see that painting? Well, I want you to re-create that same intense pain." And that was virtually the only—or, rather, the main—direction that I gave him on the film. I often use paintings like that because they allow you to communicate much more effectively than with a hundred words.

I'M OBSESSED BY THE CAMERA

The camera is very present in my films—too present at times, in fact. But I can't control that. I am truly obsessed by the body and, above all, the eye of the camera. It's what governs my directing, in the sense that it moves all the time—and in my recent films it moves even more. The camera enters and leaves the scene like an invisible character in the story. I cannot resist the temptation to move the camera. I think this comes from a desire to have a sensual relationship with the characters, in the hope that this will then mutate into a sensual relationship between the characters. In a more psychoan-alytical period of my life, I used to think that "tracking in" was the movement of the child running toward its mother while "tracking out" was the opposite, the movement of the child trying to flee.

In any case, the camera is my main center of interest on a shoot. For that reason, I need to establish prior communica-tion with the actors and technicians in order to devote the majority of my time on the set to moving the camera and choosing the lenses. I hardly ever use a zoom. I don't know why, but I find that there's something fake about its move-ment. I remember one day on the set of *The Spider Stratagem* when I felt like using a zoom for a change. I spent an hour playing with it, almost to the point of nausea. I removed it and said that I never wanted to see that kind of lens again. These days I'm starting to have a more peaceful relationship with the zoom. I use it in a very simple, almost functional way. But for many years, I looked on it as an instrument of the devil.

SEEK OUT THE MYSTERY OF THE ACTOR

I think that the secret to working well with an actor is first knowing how to choose him or her. And to succeed in that, you have to forget the character in the screenplay for a second and see whether the person in front of you intrigues you or not. This is very important because, during the shoot, it's the curiosity that you feel for this actor that will lead you to ex-plore the character in the story. Sometimes you choose an ac-tor because he or she seems to suit the written character perfectly, but you realize in the end that this isn't very inter-esting, that there's no mystery. And the driving force behind any film is, first and foremost, curiosity: the desire of the di-rector to discover each character's secret.

As for actor direction as such, I would say that I always attempt to apply the rules of cinema verité to the world of fiction. For instance, in the scene in *Last Tango* when Marlon Brando is lying in his bed and tells Maria Schneider things about his past, it was Brando who made all that up. I told him, "She's going to ask you questions; answer however you like." He started describing all those disturbing things, and as a director, I was like the audience—in other words, I couldn't tell whether he was lying or telling the truth. But that's what improvisation is for: attempting to touch the truth and show that something very true may be hidden behind the character's mask. Indeed, that was one of the first things I said to Brando. I told him that I wanted him to remove his Actors Studio mask, that I wanted to see what was behind it. We met up again a couple of years ago; we chatted, and after a while he said to me, with a mischievous smile, "So, you really think it was myself that I showed you in that film, huh?" I don't know whether he did or not, but that's what's so wonderful.

WHAT IS CINEMA?

Seemingly, a film is the setting of an idea to images. But, more secretly, for me, it has always been a way of exploring something more personal and more abstract. My films are always very different in the end from what I originally imagined. Therefore, it's a progressive process. I often compare a film to a pirate ship. It's impossible to know where it will land when you leave it free to follow the winds of creativity. Especially with someone like me, who loves blowing in the opposite direction.

Indeed, there was a time when I believed that contradiction lay at the basis of everything, that it was the driving force behind each film. And that's how I went about making *1900*, a film about the birth of Socialism financed by American dollars. In this film I mingled Hollywood actors with peasants from the Po Valley who had never seen a camera before. That amused me a great deal. When I started making films in the sixties, there was something that filmmakers called the Bazin question: "What is cinema?"* It was a sort of constant interrogation that ended up becoming the subject of each film. And then we stopped asking it because things changed. However, I have the feeling that the cinema is going through such intense upheavals now and losing so much of its uniqueness that the Bazin question is topical again and that we should once more start to wonder what cinema is.

Films: *The Grim Reaper* (*La commare secca*) (1962), *Before the Revolution* (*Prima della rivoluzione*) (1964), *Partner* (1968), *Love and Anger* (*Amore e rabbia*) (1969), *The Spider's Stratagem* (*Le strategia del ragno*) (1970), *The Conformist* (*Il conformista*) (1971), *Last Tango in Paris* (1973), *1900* (*Novecento*) (1977), *La Luna* (1979), *The Tragedy of a Ridiculous Man* (*La tragedia di un uomo ridicolo*) (1982), *The Last Emperor* (1987), *The Sheltering Sky* (1990), *Little Buddha* (1993), *Stealing Beauty* (1996), *Besieged* (1998), *Heaven and Hell* (2001)

---

*André Bazin was a postwar French film critic and theorist who co-founded the legendary *Cahiers du cinéma* and helped inspire the filmmakers of the French New Wave.

MARTIN SCORSESE
b. 1942, Queens, New York

One of the most striking things about Martin Scorsese is how fast he talks. You expect him to be brilliant, and he certainly is. But the pace at which Scorsese delivers information makes it almost intimidating to ask questions.

Our interview took place in the summer of 1997 in New York at the request of Jodie Foster, who had been designated honorary editor of an issue of Studio and wanted to have her director on Taxi Driver put through one of my master classes.

I entered Scorsese's Park Avenue production office with sweaty hands because I'm among those who consider him the most impressive filmmaker of the last twenty years. Ever since Mean Streets, he has amazed audiences and inspired a whole generation of filmmakers who have tried, usually in vain, to use the camera with his energy and precision. Some directors are great storytellers; some are excellent technicians. He is both. His encyclopedic knowledge of film history doesn't hurt either. The idea of spending a couple of hours, one-on-one, with Martin Scorsese was therefore particularly exciting—and I wasn't disappointed. He fidgeted in his chair for a few minutes at the beginning of the interview, perhaps because he was in the middle of editing Kundun at the time. I could see that his mind was still splicing images together as we chatted. But once I started asking detailed questions, Scorsese focused completely and fired off answers with such speed that I was glad I got them on a tape recorder.

■ Master Class with Martin Scorsese

I had some teaching experience at Columbia University around the time when I was making *The Color of Money* and *The Last Temptation of Christ*. I didn't show films or give lectures; I just helped graduate students by giving them advice and comments on the films they were making. What I usually found to be the most problematic with these films was their intent, what the filmmaker wanted to communicate to the audience. Now, this could make itself evident in many different ways, but it was primarily a problem of where to aim the camera, shot by shot, and how each shot builds to make a point, to show something the filmmaker wants the audience to comprehend. This can be a purely physical point—a man walks into a room and sits on a chair—or it can be a philosophical point, or a psychological point, or a thematic point—though I guess thematic would include philosophical and psychological. But you have to start with the basics, which is, Where do you aim the camera to express what you put down on paper in the script? And it's not just aiming the camera in one shot, it's the one after that, and the one after that, and how they will edit together to create what you want to say to the audience.

Of course, you may find that the biggest problem of young filmmakers is that they have nothing to say. And invariably their films will be either very unclear or very conventional and geared toward a rather commercial marketplace. So I think the first thing you need to ask yourself if you want to make a film is "Do I have anything to say?" And it doesn't necessarily have to be something literal that can be expressed through words. Sometimes you just want to communicate a feeling, an emotion. That's sufficient. And believe me, it's hard enough.

TALK ABOUT WHAT YOU KNOW

I come from a tradition in the early sixties that had to do with more personal filmmaking, with themes and subject matter that you felt more confident dealing with—about yourself, about the world you came from. That kind of cinema flourished in the seventies, but since the eighties, there's been consistently less of that in mainstream cinema. Now I even find that some of the independents are starting to show a trend toward melodrama and film noir, which indicates that they're getting their eyes set on a more commercial aspect of cinema. When I see low-budget films today, I often feel that the directors are trying to audition for the studios. You might ask, "Why do films have to be personal, anyway?" Well, of course, it's all a matter of opinion, but I tend to feel that the more singular the vision and the more personal the film, the more it can claim to be art. As a spectator, I find that when they're more personal, films last longer. You can watch them over and over again, whereas with a more commercial film, you might get bored after two showings.

So what makes a film personal? Do you have to write the script yourself to make the film yours, as the auteur theory claimed? Not necessarily. I think there's kind of a twofold situation there. I think you have to make a distinction between the directors on one side and the filmmakers on the other. The directors—and they can excel at doing that—are people who only interpret the script, who just turn it from words into images. The filmmakers, however, will be able to take somebody else's material and still manage to have a personal vision come through. They will shoot the film or direct actors in a manner that will eventually transform that film so that it becomes part of the body of work of their other films, with similar themes and approaches to material and characterization. That's what makes the whole difference between, for instance,

His Girl Friday by Howard Hawks and *Dream Life* by Sidney Sheldon. Both are studio movies; both are comedies starring Cary Grant. And yet you can watch the first one repeatedly, whereas the second one, although pleasant, will not stand a second showing. And that's also what makes the difference between a John Woo movie, which is always very personal, and, let's say, the *Batman* sequels, which may be well crafted but could have been directed by anybody.

KNOW WHAT YOU'RE TALKING ABOUT

At the risk of sounding redundant, I think the duty of a film-maker is to tell the story that he or she wants to tell, which means that you have to know what the hell you're talking about. At the very least, you have to know the feelings, the emotions you're trying to convey. It doesn't mean you can't explore, but you can only do it within the context in which the story is set.

Let's refer to one of my own pictures, *The Age of Innocence*. In that film, I took the emotions that I knew, but I set them in a world that I wanted to explore and I analyzed them in an anthropological way, to see how the trappings of that society affected these emotions—the trappings of that society being the flower arrangements, the china, the formality of body language, and how that affected emotions that I think are universal in human experience: the longing, the unfulfilled passion . . . So I took all that and put it in the pressure cooker of that particular society. But with the same characters and the same story, I think you would make a very different film if you set it in a village in, let's say, Sicily or France. So, sure, you can explore, you can experiment. But don't forget that movies cost anywhere between $1 million and $100 million. You can experiment with $1 million, but with $40 million, I don't think so. They won't give you the money again.

There are filmmakers who claim that they never know where they're going when they make a film, that they make it up as they go along. On the highest level, certainly Fellini would be the main example. But I don't quite believe that. I think he always had some idea, however abstract, of where he was going. There are also filmmakers who have a script but don't know exactly what the angles or shots of a particular scene are going to be until they get into the rehearsal of that scene, or even on the day of shooting. I know people who can work that way. I don't think I can. I need to have my shots decided in advance, even if it's all theoretical. At the very least, I need to know every evening what the first shot of the next day is going to be. In some cases, if I decide to add scenes that were not planned and that are not vital to the story, it might be fun to go there completely bare and see what I can do on the spot. But that's not what I would advocate. You need to know where you're going, and you need to have it on paper. The script is the most important thing. But don't become a slave to the script, either, because if the script is everything, you just photograph the script. The script is not everything. It's the interpretation that's everything—the visual interpretation of what you have on paper.

If you are an intuitive filmmaker, and if you have the economics under control, by all means, go ahead, take your time and make it up as you go along. I can't do it. It depends on the personality, I guess. I tried this kind of approach only once, on *New York, New York*, where I didn't quite know where I was going and tried to rely on my instincts, and I was never quite satisfied with the final outcome of that picture.

HARD CHOICES

I guess the main lesson I've learned about filmmaking is that it's a tension between knowing exactly what you want and being able to change it according to the circumstances, or taking advantage of something more interesting. So the whole problem is being able to know what is essential, what you absolutely cannot change, mustn't change, and what you can be more flexible on.

Sometimes you go to a location and the location is very different from what you had in your mind when you imagined the shots you were going to make there. So what do you do? Do you try to get a new location, or do you change your shots? In other cases, you can make up the shots from the location. I did it both ways. Sometimes I went to the location first and designed the shots from there, and sometimes I decided on the shots beforehand and then tried to make them work within the constraints of the location. I tend to go more for this second option, though.

Working out a theoretical shot list includes camera placement and decisions on who is in the frame and who isn't. Are the actors shot in separate frames, or are they in each other's frames? Or are they singles, and if they're singles, what size are they? That sort of thing. Are there camera movements? On what lines? Where? Why? Ideally, those theories can be applied in any location. Very often, though, there are walls and ceilings you have to deal with. Except in a studio situation, of course. But in a studio, you usually have only enough money to build three walls, and you cannot do a 180-degree shot, for instance. Now, if you feel there *has* to be a 180-degree shot on that set, you have to have it. And so maybe you spend more money to get a fourth wall, and maybe you'll have to lose certain scenes of that film to remain in the budget. You have to know what's important, what cannot be changed, and you have to fight for it. But you mustn't be stubborn, you mustn't say no to everything that creates a change. Because if you do, you're not allowing for the life around the camera and the set to come through. And it shows on the film. Sometimes an accident or a last-minute change can create something unexpected and magical. And sometimes you can be so stubborn in what you want that the life you create on film becomes rigid and formal. You have to be aware of that.

A LANGUAGE TO (RE)INVENT?

Is there a grammar in filmmaking, the same way there is a grammar in literature? Well, sure there is. And it's been given to us twice. As Jean-Luc Godard said, we've had two main teachers in film history: D. W. Griffith in the silent era and Orson Welles in the talking era. So of course there are basic rules. But even today, people are still struggling with new ways of telling stories through film, and they're still using the same tools—establishing shots, medium shots, close-ups—but not necessarily with the same intent. And it's the juxtaposition of these shots in the editing process that is creating new emotions or, more precisely, a new way to communicate certain feelings to the audience.

The first examples that come to mind are films by Oliver Stone, such as *Natural Born Killers* or *Nixon*. In *Nixon*, for instance, there is a sequence in which the President is hallucinating: you have a shot of his wife talking to him, and then you cut to a black-and-white shot, and then you go back to the wife and you can still hear her talking—except on the screen, she's not saying anything. This is really interesting because Stone found a way to create an emotion and to create a psychological state purely through editing. You have a close-up of a person who is not saying anything, and the shot is still creating an emotion. David Lynch is another filmmaker whose experimentation with the language of film is very interesting. In many ways, the grammar of film is up for grabs. Anyone can try a new way of juxtaposing shots to tell a story.

I guess the film I experimented on the most was probably *Goodfellas*. But then again, I'm not sure I would call that experimenting, as the style was mainly based on *Citizen Kane*'s "March of Time" sequence and the first few minutes of Truffaut's *Jules and Jim*. In the latter film, every frame is just filled with information, beautiful information, and there's a narration which tells you one thing when, in fact, the image shows you something else . . . It's very, very rich, and that sort of richness of detail is what I played with in *Goodfellas*. So it was nothing new, really. But what was new, I felt, was the exhilaration of the narration juxtaposed to the images to create the emotion of that lifestyle, of being a young gangster. The other film on which I experimented a lot was *King of Comedy*, but mostly in terms of acting style—and, of course, because there were no camera movements at all, which, for me, was very unusual.

SEEING LIFE THROUGH A 25-MILLIMETER LENS

As with all directors, there are certain tools that I like to use and others that I am not so fond of. For example, I don't mind using a zoom lens, which many directors hate. But there are two things I don't like about it: first, the overuse of zoom for shock effect, which is something that Mario Bava did originally in the sixties.* It still works when you see his movies, but, of course, it's a particular genre. The main problem with the zoom lens is the lack of hard element in the lens, so the image is not as crystal clear as you would have with a prime lens.

When I work with Michael Ballhaus at the camera, we often use a zoom lens, but we use it together with camera move-

*Mario Bava (1914–1980) was an Italian director who acquired cult status in the sixties because of the exceptional creativity and refinement he showed in making cheap genre films, his specialty being grisly horror films.

ment to change the size of the frame, so we're disguising the zoom as the camera's moving to get closer to an object or farther away from it. As a rule, however, I prefer wide-angle lenses. I like 25 millimeters and wider, and that has mostly to do with Orson Welles, John Ford, and even some movies by Anthony Mann. These are movies that I grew up watching, and they used the wide angle to create a sort of expressionistic look which I guess I liked very much. Which is also why I like contemporary Polish cinema, where directors use the wide angle a lot, not for obvious distortion but for crispness and for a dramatic use of the lines. The way the lines converge in a wide-angle-lens image is more dramatic, I think.

When I made *New York, New York*, I shot most of it with a 32-millimeter lens because I wanted a flatter look, like the films of the late forties.* Musicals were a little different, though, because although they were going for that flatter look, they would use wide-angle lenses up to 25 or 18 millimeters, shooting from a low angle to get the ceiling for dramatic effect. And so, anyway, I used a 32-millimeter lens to get the look of these films of the late forties, where characters were mainly composed from below the knee up. That's what I tried in that film.

Originally, I also wanted to try a 1.33:1 aspect ratio, but we wouldn't have been able to get it projected properly, so we shot it in 1.66:1, which is the current standard format.† I don't particularly like to use long lenses because I feel they make the image look indefinite. I like the way other people use them—for instance, David Fincher in *Seven*. And of

---

*Wide-angle lenses give more depth of field, more perspective, more richness to the shot, which is the opposite of a "flat" look. Shooting from a low angle—with the camera below eye level, looking up at the characters—increases that effect.

†The aspect ratio defines the format of the frame. A square picture has a 1:1 ratio. A TV screen has a 1.25:1 ratio, meaning that the horizontal part of the screen is 1.25 times longer than the vertical part. Until the fifties, most films were shot in a 1.33:1 ratio. Today, the standard is either 1.66:1 or 1.85:1. Cinemascope is 2.35:1.

course Akira Kurosawa always used them beautifully. But when I use a long lens, it has to be with a very specific purpose. For instance, there's one scene in *Raging Bull* that I shot only with long lenses. I believe it's the second Sugar Ray fight, and we had rippling flames in front of the lens to distort the image. So sometimes the use of bits of imagery through long lenses like that can be very good. But very often I find that a lot of people who don't really know how to shoot just put two people off in the distance, have them walk toward the camera, and shoot it all with a long lens. You can get it easily that way, but for me the image always seems undirected.

ACTORS MUST BE FREE—OR THINK THEY ARE

There's no secret to directing actors, really. I mean, it depends on the director. Some directors get great performances with actors even though they are very cold with them, very demanding, and even nasty at times.

My impression of working with actors is that it's good if you have actors that you like as people. Well, at least, you have to like certain aspects of them. I think that's the way Griffith worked. He really liked the actors he directed. But we've also heard all the stories of Hitchcock and how he hated actors. I don't believe that entirely, though. I think it's just a funny thing to say. But no matter how he behaved, he got great performances out of them. Fritz Lang was very tough with actors and got great performances from them too—or at least he got what he needed.

Personally, I have to like the actors I'm working with, and I try to give them as much freedom as possible to make the scenes come alive. Of course, "freedom" is a relative term on a movie set because there are so many constraints. So, really, you have to give the actors the impression that they're free within the schematics of a scene. And sometimes these can be the schematics of three feet of space. But I think the actor needs to feel free to come up with something interesting. I don't like to reel in an actor with a certain light or a certain lens. I've had to do it sometimes, of course, and I've been lucky because I've worked with actors who could be free and still hit their marks correctly. I guess you can tell from my movies that most of the time, my shots are very precise. But I always try to work it out with the director of photography so that the actors eventually have space to move.

There's a certain freedom in *Goodfellas*, as it's mostly medium shots, where the actors have room to move. But that's the world these characters live in. It's not a world of close-ups. They have people around them all the time, and what they do always affects the world around them. So you have to shoot it in medium shots.

It's important not to restrict actors. But, on the other hand, I cannot let actors give me something that I don't want. On a film like *Casino*, there was a lot of improvisation, which is fine. If an actor feels really comfortable playing that character in that world, I let him improvise within a given scene, and I cover it in a pretty straightforward manner: medium shots, close-ups . . . When you do that, the world is pretty much created by the actors. I place them in the frame, and the set around them is part of their life, but they bring the life to it. When that happens, and when it goes in the direction you wanted, it can be incredibly rewarding. Often on that film, I found myself sitting behind the camera not as a director, but as an audience member. I got so involved in watching that it was like I was watching a film somebody else was directing. And when you get that feeling, you know you're on to something good.

WHOM DO YOU MAKE FILMS FOR?

Some directors make films strictly for the audience. Others, like Steven Spielberg or Alfred Hitchcock, make them for the audience and for themselves. Hitchcock was great at doing that; he knew exactly how to play the audience. So you could say that Hitchcock made only suspense movies, which is true in a sense, but there was a psychology behind his films that was so personal that it made him a great filmmaker. These were personal films disguised as thrillers, really.

As for me, well, I make films for myself. I'm thinking and knowing that there will be an audience out there, of course. But how big an audience, I don't know. Some people will see the film; some will appreciate it; some will even see it repeatedly, but certainly not everybody. So I find that the best way for me to work is to make a film as if I'm the audience.

As I sometimes work for studios, I have my films tested by an audience to see how they react. I find that interesting in terms of finding out the ABC's of what you're doing. You find out if certain things are not communicated, if certain things are confusing and need to be cleared up, if there are length problems or redundancies, that sort of thing. But as far as the audience saying, "I don't like the people you're showing me, I wouldn't go see this movie," well . . . that's life! When the film comes out, there will be publicity on it, and people who go see it will know what to expect. But in a test audience, of course, there are going to be many people who couldn't care less. And so you have to know which comments to listen to and which to ignore. That causes problems with the studio, of course, because they want everything addressed.

The only film I made particularly for an audience was *Cape Fear*. But this was a genre film, a thriller, and when you do that there are certain rules you must follow so that the audience reacts in certain ways: suspense, fear, excitement, laughter . . . But still, let me put it this way: the skeleton of that film I did for the audience; the rest was for myself.

MAKE A POINT—BUT ONLY ONCE

There are many different kinds of mistakes that I think a director must try to avoid at all costs. The first that comes to mind is redundancy—making the point of a film over and over again, either emotionally or intellectually. Well, emotionally, you can get away with it sometimes, because the emotion can become intense enough to become something else. But in terms of a message, whether it's a political message or just the underlying theme of the film, I sometimes see films in which, at the end, a character will, either virtually or literally, make a speech or have a line of dialogue where he will explain that the film title means or even explain what the film was all about. And that, I feel, is the worst thing you can do. I'm not sure I've avoided that myself. But I've certainly tried.

Films: *Who's That Knocking at My Door?* (1968), *Boxcar Bertha* (1972), *Mean Streets* (1973), *Alice Doesn't Live Here Anymore* (1975), *Taxi Driver* (1976), *New York, New York* (1977), *Raging Bull* (1980), *The King of Comedy* (1983), *After Hours* (1985), *The Color of Money* (1986), *The Last Temptation of Christ* (1988), *New York Stories* (1989), *Goodfellas* (1990), *Cape Fear* (1991), *The Age of Innocence* (1993), *Casino* (1995), *Kundun* (1997), *Bringing Out the Dead* (1999), *Gangs of New York* (2001)

WIM WENDERS
b. 1945, Düsseldorf, Germany

If the seventies are regarded as the golden age of innovative movies, then it can also be said that worldwide cinema became more standardized in the eighties. But a few directors kept thinking about new ways of making films, and Wim Wenders was definitely the leader of that group. After the critically acclaimed but barely noticed The American Friend *and* Lightning over Water, *Wenders made* Paris, Texas *and proved that audiences were still hungry for something new. Somewhat experimental and very poetic, the film broke traditional rules of storytelling. A whole generation of filmmakers followed in Wenders's footsteps, but he chose to go in a different direction. He surprised everybody with the truly magnificent* Wings of Desire, *for which he hired Henri Alekan, the veteran director of photography who had worked on Jean Cocteau's* Beauty and the Beast *back in the forties.*

A director who is always exploring is bound to make mistakes; that's part of the game. Some of Wenders's later films, such as The End of Violence *or* The Million Dollar Hotel, *are somehow less interesting than much of his earlier work. Nevertheless, he once again took everybody by surprise with the amazing documentary* Buena Vista Social Club. *So who knows what to expect next from Wim Wenders?*

We met at the Cannes Film Festival, and in the midst of that crazy circus, it was refreshing to see how he took his time to think his answers over. He went so far in his analyses that I sometimes felt more like a psychiatrist than a journalist, but such a response should have been expected from a man who has clearly made it a rule to question everything.

▨ Master Class with Wim Wenders

For some years now, I have been teaching filmmaking at the Munich Film School, where I studied in the early seventies. I try to make my teaching as practical as possible because theoretical classes, like those that I took at the time, were never much use to me. In fact, my true apprenticeship as a director took place a few years later, when I worked as a critic. I think that there are two particular ways of learning to make films. The first, of course, is to make them. The second is to write reviews. Writing forces you to take your analysis further, by trying to define and explain in a concrete way (for others and above all for yourself) why a film works or fails.

The main difference between criticism and a theoretical class is that when you write criticism, there's a direct relationship between you and the screen: you're speaking about what you have seen. In a theoretical class, there's an intermediary—the teacher—who explains to you what you need to see. In other words, what he himself has seen or, in the worst cases, what he has been told he should see. It unavoidably distorts the process of comprehension a great deal, and this is why I don't recommend this as a way of learning.

THE DESIRE TO TELL A STORY

What strikes me most about students and young filmmakers today is that they no longer start out by making short films but shoot commercials or music videos instead. Of course, this is a result of the evolution of the audiovisual industry. They're living in a culture where the priorities are different from my day's. However, the problem with music videos and commercials, as opposed to short films, is that the notion of storytelling suffers a great deal. I have the impression that this generation, through working with images that have a totally different primal function, is losing the notion of what story-telling means. Telling a story is no longer the main goal or the primary impulse. And though I don't wish to generalize, I have the feeling that young directors are, above all, aiming to accomplish something new. They feel that they must impress audiences with the novelty of their work, and at times a visual gag can become a sufficient reason to make a film. However, I believe that, above all, the director's duty is to have something to say: he or she needs to tell a story.

I reached this conclusion only recently; in fact, when I started out, I didn't give a damn about stories either. For me, at first, the only thing that counted was the image—the appropriateness of an image or a situation. But never the story. It was an alien notion. In a pinch, the sum of several situations could form something that you could call a story, but I never saw it as a proposition with a start, middle, and end.

It was while making *Paris, Texas* that I had a sort of revelation. I realized that the story was like a river and that if you dared to set sail on it, and if you trusted the river, then the boat would be carried along toward something magical. Up until then, I had always fought against the current. I had remained in a small pond on the side because I lacked confidence. On that particular film, I realized that the stories are there, that they exist without us. There's no need to create them, really, because humankind brings them to life. You simply have to let yourself be carried along by them.

Ever since that day, telling a story has become an increasingly powerful goal in my approach to cinema while that of making beautiful images has moved into the background and has even become an obstacle at times. At first, the greatest compliment that anyone could pay me was to tell me that I had made some beautiful images. Today, if someone tells me that, I feel that the film is a failure.

MAKING A FILM: WHY? AND FOR WHOM?

There are two ways of making a film, or, if you prefer, two reasons for doing it. The first consists of having a very clear idea and expressing it through the film. The second consists of making the film to discover what you are attempting to say. Personally, I have always been torn between these two approaches. And I have tried them both.

I have shot films with precisely constructed screenplays that I have followed to the letter, and I have made others in which the whole experience was without limits and outside the initial idea. This kind of film is a sort of adventure in itself, and I think it remains my favorite approach. I like to have fairly open experiences where I'm able to explore and change the course of the story as I go along. This is clearly a privileged way of working that implies shooting the film in sequence. But the few times I was able to do it, I found this much more satisfying than the other approach, in which you merely carry out decisions made beforehand.

The way in which you make the film therefore depends a great deal on the *reason* you make it. As for knowing *for whom* you're making it, I think that someone who shoots films for the images alone does so for his own benefit. After all, the perfection of an image, the power of an image, is an extremely personal notion, whereas telling a story is, by definition, an act of communication. Someone who attempts to tell a story necessarily needs an audience. And as I've gradually turned towards storytelling, I've started making my films for the audience. There again, I could never define this audience. I consider it a gathering wider than my circle of friends. Therefore, I believe that in general, I make a film for my friends—in other words, primarily for those who work on the film. They form my initial audience, and I try to ensure that the film interests them. Then come my friends in the larger meaning of the term. And finally the general public that my friends, in a way, represent.

THE NEED TO LIVE OUT THE SCENE

When I made my first films, I would spend every evening painstakingly preparing the way in which I was going to shoot the next day's scenes. I would make drawings almost as detailed as those of a storyboard, and when I arrived on the set, I knew exactly what shots I was going to film and how. I'd usually begin by preparing the frame, and then I'd position the actors, telling them where to stand and how to move within it. But, little by little, I felt that this was becoming a trap. And then, just before shooting *Paris, Texas,* I had the chance to direct a stage play. And this experience immensely changed my way of working, probably because it forced me to concentrate much more on the actor's work and therefore allowed me to better understand and appreciate it.

Since then, I have done the opposite of what I used to do. In other words, I find my scene construction in the action. I arrive on the set without any preconceived ideas about the shots I'm going to film, and only after working with the actors, after making them move around the set, do I start to think about where I'm going to set up the camera. This process takes much more time, of course, because you can't light the set until you decide on the shot breakdown, but I know now that I need to "live out" the scene before shooting it. Even during scouting, I find that I can't look at an empty set and start to think about the way I'm going to film it. I don't have that gift—or, rather, I don't have it anymore.

THERE ISN'T JUST ONE WAY OF FILMING

Each director has his own filmic grammar, a grammar that he learned from someone or that he has invented for himself. Originally, my grammar came from American movies, more precisely, from the films of Anthony Mann and Nicholas Ray. But eventually I sensed that I was becoming imprisoned within certain dogmatic rules, and I started to reinvent them. Other directors learn by working as assistants to great directors. I didn't have that kind of experience until recently, and it was a great lesson. In 1995 I worked on Michelangelo Antonioni's film *Beyond the Clouds* as a sort of assistant. Of course, I had a very different approach from that of an ordinary assistant director, first, because I had contributed to the screenplay, and second, because I had already directed a number of films. As a result, when I arrived on the set of his film in the morning, I couldn't prevent myself from thinking about what I would do with the same actors and sets if it were my own film. And I think that virtually each time Antonioni was getting ready to shoot a scene, I was thinking to myself, "This isn't going to work. It's not possible. The way this scene is written, you can't start off with a tracking shot." And, of course, I was nearly always wrong. He would shoot the scene in his own way, and it would work. It was totally different from what I would have done with the same material, but it was just as valid.

This experience softened some of the dogmatic and rigid ideas that I used to have about directing. For instance, I had always refused to shoot anything with a zoom lens. It was forbidden. The zoom was an enemy. I had a theory according to which the camera had to work like a human eye, and since the eye cannot zoom in or out and since you need to get closer to see something in greater detail, I preferred tracking shots to zooms. Much to my horror, Antonioni shot virtually everything with a zoom lens. And I was impressed by the result at times.

Similarly, I had always refused to shoot with two cameras because I think that the second usually becomes an obstacle for the first. Antonioni, on the other hand, insisted on having at least three. And, once again, most of the time this worked perfectly. I therefore came out of this experience with a much greater feeling of freedom in relation to directing. And I now think that all directors should try it, to see how another filmmaker would shoot the same scene. This opens doors, offers new options, and allows you to realize that there are always alternatives to what you do. And even if it is a little unsettling at first, I think it's a wonderful way of bringing about changes in your work.

SECRETS, DANGERS, MISTAKES

The main secret that I have discovered probably regards actors. When you start making films, actors are generally what scare you the most, and you desperately attempt to find a way to direct them. But the secret, of course, is that there isn't one particular way. Each actor has his or her own methods, needs, and means of self-expression. There are as many methods as actors. And in the end, all you can do as a director is put the actors sufficiently at their ease so that they no longer perform, so they no longer pretend to be someone else. You choose actors for what they are, so make sure that they can be themselves. Of course, this implies that they have sufficient confidence in the situation that you throw them into.

The greatest danger that I'd warn any director about is the balance between his own weight and that of the film. The smaller the budget, the easier it is to control the film. The larger it is, the more you become a slave to it. Beyond a certain threshold, your ambition can turn against you and cause your downfall.

Finally, regarding the mistakes that a director should never make: there are a great many, and I think I've made them all. But the greatest is probably to think that you need to show everything you're trying to say. Where violence is concerned, for example, no one seems able to find any alternative other than to show it, but in fact the cinema often achieves its greatest impact by refusing to show what it is attempting to evoke. Never forget that.

Films: *Summer in the City* (1970), *The Goalie's Anxiety at the Penalty Kick* (*Die Angst des Tormannes beim Elfmeter*) (1971), *The Scarlet Letter* (*Der scharlachrote Buchstabe*) (1973), *Alice in the Cities* (*Alice in den Städten*) (1974), *The Wrong Move* (*Falsche Bewegung*) (1974), *Kings of the Road* (*Im Lauf der Zeit*) (1976), *The American Friend* (*Der Amerikanische Freund*) (1977), *Nick's Movie* (*Lightning over Water*) (1980), *The State of Things* (*Der Stand der Dinge*) (1982), *Hammett* (1982), *Paris, Texas* (1984), *Tokyo-Ga* (1985), *Wings of Desire* (*Der Himmel über Berlin*) (1987), *Notebook on Cities and Clothes* (*Aufzeichnungen zu Kleidern und Städten*) (1989), *Until the End of the World* (*Bis ans Ende der Welt*) (1991), *Faraway, So Close!* (*In weiter Ferne, so nah!*) (1993), *Lisbon Story* (1995), *The End of Violence* (*Am Ende der Gewalt*) (1997), *Buena Vista Social Club* (1999), *The Million Dollar Hotel* (2000)

DREAM WEAVERS

Pedro Almodóvar
Tim Burton
David Cronenberg
Jean-Pierre Jeunet
David Lynch

Signature is what makes a truly great director: something inherent to a filmmaker's work that is instantly identifiable, in the same way that a van Gogh painting cannot be mistaken for anyone else's. This indefinable element is possessed by all the filmmakers in this book, but it might be most true of these five directors, who, through their persistent obsessions and their striking visual styles, have managed to draw audiences on a continuing journey into the deepest parts of their imagination.

PEDRO ALMODÓVAR

b. 1951, Calzada de Calatrava, Ciudad Real, Spain

Pedro Almodóvar is the phoenix of Spanish cinema, raising Spain's film industry out of its own ashes. Before he surprised audiences in the early nineties with Women on the Verge of a Nervous Breakdown (Mujeres al borde de un ataque de nervios) *and* Tie Me Up! Tie Me Down! (Átame), *everybody thought Buñuel had taken the nation's visual talent with him to the grave. Then came Almodóvar's flamboyantly hilarious, politically incorrect, and incredibly generous-spirited films, which established his voice and made his work a point of reference for moviegoers the world over.*

I met Almodóvar as he was releasing All About My Mother, *one of his most personal—and possibly one of his best—films, for which he would later receive the Best Director Prize at the Cannes Film Festival and the Oscar for Best Foreign Film at the Academy Awards. Like the characters in his films, Pedro Almodóvar likes to dress in flashy colors, but his personality is much more reserved. Sitting behind his desk in an office that looks like a museum dedicated to pop culture, Almodóvar took his role as teacher quite seriously. He listened to my questions attentively, often pondered a while before answering, and sometimes double-checked with his translator to make sure his response had not been distorted. But there is absolutely nothing academic or dogmatic in the way Pedro Almodóvar approaches cinema. In fact, it's clear that he makes films mainly because he has a very good time doing so.*

Master Class with Pedro Almodóvar

Although I have had many offers, I never wanted to teach film. The reason for this is that, in my opinion, film can be learned but not taught. It is an art where technique is less important than approach. It's an entirely personal form of expression. You can ask any technician to show you the "conventional" way of shooting a given scene, but if you shoot it according to those instructions, there will always be something missing in the end. And that thing is you—your point of view, your means of self-expression. Directing is a purely personal experience. Which is why I think you must discover film language by yourself and you must discover yourself through that language. If you want to learn film, maybe a shrink would be more useful than a teacher!

TO LEARN FILMMAKING, MAKE FILMS

Once or twice, I have met with students, mostly in American universities, to answer questions about my films. What struck me was that my cinema clearly didn't resemble what their teachers had taught them. I could tell that they were lost and confused, not because of the complexity of my answers but, on the contrary, because of their simplicity. They had imagined that I would reveal all kinds of precisely and carefully thought-out rules. But the truth is, there are either too many rules or too few. And I know hundreds of examples proving that one can make a good film by breaking all the rules. I remember that when I shot my first film, I had major problems that forced me to take several shots of the same scene over a whole year. Consequently, at the start of the scene, the actress has short hair; in the next shot, her hair is medium long; and, in the third shot, very long. On noticing this while cutting the film, I thought the audience would howl, because this went against the most basic rule of all, that of the match cut. But no one noticed a thing. Ever. And that was a great lesson for me. It proved that in the end, no one gives a damn about technical errors as long as the film tells an interesting story with a genuine point of view. That is why my advice to anyone who wants to make films is to make them, even if they don't know how. They'll learn by doing it, in the most vibrant and organic way possible.

The vital thing, of course, is to have something to say. The problem with the younger generation in relation to this is that they have grown up in a world where the image has become omnipresent and omnipotent. Since their early years, they have been fed a diet of music videos and commercials. These are not forms that I'm particularly fond of, but their visual fertility is undeniable. So young filmmakers today have a culture and mastery of the image much greater than they would have had just twenty years ago. However, because of this, they also have an approach to the cinema that emphasizes the form rather than the content, and I believe that this can be harmful in the long run. In fact, I believe that technique is an illusion. Personally, I know that the more I learn, the less I want to use what I learn. It's almost like a hindrance, and I aim more and more for simplicity. I virtually always use only lenses with very short focal lengths or very long ones, and I rarely use any camera movement. I've reached the point where I almost force myself to write a thesis to justify the briefest tracking shot!

DON'T BORROW—STEAL!

You can also learn cinema, to a lesser extent, by watching films. Here, however, the danger is that you might fall into the trap of the *hommage*. You watch how certain master filmmakers shoot a scene, and then you try to copy that in your own films. If you do it out of pure admiration, it can't work. The only valid reason to do it is if you find the solution to one of your own problems in someone else's film and this influence then becomes an active element in your film. One could say that the first approach—the tribute—is borrowing, whereas the second is theft. But for me, only theft is justifiable. If it's necessary, one should never hesitate; every filmmaker does it.

If you take John Ford's *The Quiet Man*, you can clearly see that the scene in which John Wayne kisses Maureen O'Hara for the first time, with the door opening and the wind rushing into the room, is an idea that comes directly from Douglas Sirk.* As directors, Sirk and Ford are diametrically opposed, and Ford's films have nothing in common with Sirk's flamboyant melodramas. But in this particular scene, Ford needed to express the wild animal energy of John Wayne and turned directly to Sirk to find the answer to his problem. This was no *hommage*; it was plain and simple theft, but justified theft.

Personally, my greatest source of inspiration is probably Hitchcock. And what I've taken most from him are colors, first because these are colors that remind me of my childhood, and also—and this is probably connected—because they are the colors that correspond to my notion of what a story is.

CONTROL IS AN ILLUSION

I think that it is important for a filmmaker to abandon the illusion that he can—or even worse, *must*—control everything in relation to his film. In reality, to make a film, you need a crew made up of human beings. And human beings cannot be controlled one hundred percent. You can choose the frame, but when it comes to shooting, everything is in the

---

*Almodóvar appears to be referring to *Written on the Wind* (1957), one of the most "flamboyant" melodramas directed by Sirk.

hands of the camera operator. You can talk for hours and hours about the light you want, but in the end, only the gaffer decides what the light will be like. And it doesn't matter. First, because this struggle that pits you against the limits of your control is, in itself, very creative; and second, because there are areas in which your control remains complete—areas that you must concentrate on.

There are three such areas: the text; the actors' performance; and the choice of the main color, the one that will dominate in the sets, costumes, and the film's general tone. My self-expression comes to the fore in these three fields, and I try to take it as far as possible. But the notion of control is really quite relative on a set. And this holds true at every level. For example, unless you write a part with a specific actor in mind, which I don't like to do, it's impossible to find an actor who is a perfect match for the character in the screenplay. So the best thing is to choose the actor who is the closest to the physical characteristics required and then rewrite the character according to the age, accent, origins, and, above all, the personality of the actor you have chosen. You do this in a progressive way, during rehearsals, so that when you come to shoot the film, you have the impression that you have found the ideal actor for the part. This is an illusion, of course, but it helps.

Finally, to take these ideas one step further, it's hard to say what degree of control one can have over the film's basic idea. Most of the time, I know that each film needs to be made at that specific point in time, but I could never explain why. And I never know what the film is really about. Often I understand it only when the film is completed. And sometimes I don't understand it until I hear people's comments. To be honest, I suppose that I have always known it, but subconsciously. During shooting, every decision that I make is governed entirely by my instinct. I act as if I know exactly where I'm heading, but in fact, I don't. I don't know the path, or, rather, I recognize it only when I see it. However, I don't know the destination.

Cinema, therefore, is above all an exploration. You make films for purely personal reasons, to discover things for yourself. It's an intimate process that, ironically, occurs via a means of expression that must aim at the widest audience possible. It's something that you do for others but which will only work if you're convinced that it's solely for you.

THE MAGIC OF THE SET

The set is both the most concrete and the most unstable part of making a film. It's the point where all decisions are made and also where anything can happen, for better or for worse. People often talk about "pre-visualizing" things, and some directors claim to have the whole film in their minds ahead of time. Even so, a great number of things arise only at the last minute, when all the elements of a scene are brought together on the set.

The first example that comes to mind is the car accident scene in *All About My Mother* (*Todo sobre mi madre*). At first I had planned to film it with a stunt man and end with a long tracking shot of the mother running along the street, in the rain, toward her dying son. But when we started rehearsing the scene, I didn't like what the stunt man was suggesting. And as I thought about it, I realized that the tracking shot was far too similar to one that I had already used at the end of *Law of Desire*. So I decided, on the spur of the moment, to shoot the whole scene differently—in other words, with a subjective camera. The camera films the boy's point of view, passes over the hood of the car, and then crashes to the ground, and we see the mother running toward it. In the end, this is probably one of the most powerful sequences in the film. And yet it was not planned.

This kind of intuitive, improvised, or accidental decision is what makes the set so magical. Otherwise, as a rule, the way I work on a given scene is that I work the frame first. I set the camera and ask the actors to do "mechanical" movements. Then, once the frame is set, I send the crew out and work alone with the actors.

I could try to talk about actor direction, but frankly, I think that is a typical example of what cannot be taught. It's a totally personal thing that implies being able to listen to others, understand them, and understand oneself. It's inexplicable. In any case, I rehearse one last time with the actors and make final adjustments to their lines, usually by shortening them to get straight to the point. Then I shoot the scene, and I try several tones. I don't cover the scene in the classical sense, by using different angles. What I do, however, is point the scene in a different direction with each take. Sometimes I ask the actors to do the scene again faster or slower. Sometimes I redo it in a more comical or more dramatic tone. And afterwards, in the cutting room, I choose the tone that best suits the film as a whole. Strangely, most of the ideas that I get on the set are comic ones, and I'm often torn between the fear of harming the film's serious tone and the frustration of missing out on the comic moments. Consequently, this method allows me to try out everything and choose later.

LEONE, LYNCH, AND WIDE SCREEN

I don't really have any fads or tics in my directing. However, there is something particular to my last two films. First of all, I am using new kinds of lenses, known as primes, that I am extremely pleased with, both because of the density that they give to colors and, above all—and this may surprise you—because of the texture that they give to hazy objects in the background. Then, and this is the most important thing, I now shoot in anamorphic wide screen, with a much broader image format.* Anamorphic isn't an easy format to use. It creates certain problems, notably with close-ups. To shoot close-ups in wide screen, you have to be much closer to the faces, and you get so close at times that it can be dangerous because there is no possibility of lying. This forces you to ask yourself what you're really saying in a close-up. You need very good actors and they need something real to perform; otherwise, everything will fall apart.

I say this and yet, at the same time, I could easily provide a counterexample of everything that I'm saying, with Sergio Leone. The way in which Leone filmed very tight close-ups in his Westerns was totally artificial. I'm sorry, but personally, I find that Charles Bronson is an actor who expresses nothing at all. And the intensity given off by the close-ups of his face during the gunfight sequences is totally fake. However, audiences adored it.

The opposite example would be David Lynch. When he films certain objects in close-ups, he manages to give these shots genuine suggestive power. Not only are the images faultless from an aesthetic viewpoint, but they are also full of mystery. His approach is close to mine except that since I am more fascinated by actors, I like to film faces, while Lynch, who was trained in the plastic arts, is clearly more interested in objects.

---

*Anamorphic wide screen is the same thing as Cinemascope, film with a 2.35:1 aspect ratio. It is called "anamorphic" because of the complex optical process used to compress a rectangular image onto a square piece of film.

MUST A DIRECTOR WRITE TO BE AN AUTEUR?

Something strange has happened in the cinema over the last fifty years. In the old days, the director didn't need to write the screenplay film in order to be a film's creator. Filmmakers like John Ford, Howard Hawks, or John Huston didn't write screenplays, and yet they truly managed to be the authors of their films and of their work, in the broadest possible sense.

Today, I think that there is a genuine difference between directors who write and those who don't. People like Atom Egoyan and the Coen brothers, for instance, could never make the films that they make if they didn't write them themselves. Martin Scorsese is a little different. True, he doesn't write himself, but he participates in an extremely active manner in the writing and makes all the important decisions. Consequently, there is a genuine continuity in his work, a genuine balance between his films. Stephen Frears, on the other hand, doesn't write. He simply turns preexisting screenplays into films. And, as a result, his career is much more chaotic and his body of work less coherent. He is totally dependent on the screenplays he chooses, and I think that he would gain a lot by writing himself.

However, the problem comes more from the writers than the directors. Fifty years ago, the greatest novelists of the day wrote screenplays for Hollywood: William Faulkner, Dashiell Hammett, Raymond Chandler, Lillian Hellman . . . And I think that they fought a lot harder than today's writers do to impose their ideas. When I read the memoirs of Anita Loos, I'm amazed to see that the ingenuity she used to get around the ridiculous demands of the studios was as great as that required to write a terrific screenplay.

The problem today is that writers no longer seem to have such courage, and they end up writing to please the studios and the producers. When the text finally reaches the director, a dozen intermediaries who have all given their own opinions have already reworked it. Nothing original can emerge from such a process. To avoid this, most directors therefore prefer to write themselves. However, this is a stopgap solution. Ideally, a director should find a writer who is a sort of soul mate, and their relationship should be similar to a marriage. This was clearly the case for Scorsese and Schrader on *Taxi Driver*. They formed an ideal partnership. They were what every director and screenwriter should be: two sides of the same coin.

Films: *Pepi, Luci, Bom (Pepi, Luci, Bom & otras chicas del montón)* (1980), *Labyrinth of Passion (Laberinto de pasiones)* (1982), *Dark Habits (Entre tinieblas)* (1984), *What Have I Done to Deserve This? (¿Que he hecho yo para merecer esto?)* (1985), *Matador* (1986), *Law of Desire (La ley del deseo)* (1987), *Women on the Verge of a Nervous Breakdown (Mujeres al borde de un ataque de nervios)* (1988), *Tie Me Up! Tie Me Down! (Átame)* (1990), *High Heels (Tacones lejanos)*, *Kika* (1993), *The Flower of My Secret (La flor de mi secreto)* (1995), *Live Flesh (Carne trémula)* (1997), *All About My Mother (Todo sobre mi madre)* (1999)

TIM BURTON

b. 1958, Burbank, California

Although I've met many adults who have remained children in-side, I've never met anyone quite like Tim Burton. It is somehow comforting to think that a man who draws skulls on his knuck-les during an interview has Hollywood studio executives beg-ging to produce his next film. But if they do, it's because few filmmakers of Burton's generation possess such wild imagina-tion and so much controlled talent. There is something of a Walt Disney in him, but a Walt Disney whose idea of a cheer-ful place is a cave filled with bats.

In his first short film, Vincent, Burton told the story of a young man who dreamed of becoming the prince of darkness but was trapped in a suburban home in sunny California. Like that kid, Burton grew up fascinated by vampires, zombies, and cheap horror films. As a result, he has become the perfect spokesman for weirdness as embodied by all sorts of hilariously marginal creatures.

Through pure visual poetry, his films always manage to show the beauty inside the beast. Like magic, however, poetry is not something one can easily explain. But Tim Burton did his best at explaining how he works, punctuating his answers with ges-tures, faces, sound effects, and giggles that I unfortunately could not reproduce on paper. I hope one can read the joy and enthusiasm between the lines.

▨ Master Class with Tim Burton

The way I got into filmmaking has more to do with chance than anything else. I originally wanted to get into animation, and after a few internships here and there, I entered the Disney animation team. But it quickly became pretty obvious that I didn't quite fit into the Disney style. Also, this was a pretty dark moment for the studio: Disney had just made *The Fox and the Hound* and *The Black Cauldron*, both of which had been big commercial failures, and everybody felt the studio was going to permanently close down the animation department. It was like a sinking ship; there wasn't really anybody in charge anymore. So I was pretty much left to myself for a whole year, and I started working on a lot of personal ideas.

One of those projects was a story called *Vincent*. Originally, I saw it as a book for children, but since I was at Disney, I figured, why not use the equipment and turn it into a short animated film? I did that, and the success of it encouraged me to make a live-action short, *Frankenwilly*, that some people liked so much that they offered to let me direct *Pee-Wee's Big Adventure*. To this day, I still can't believe things happened so easily. I think I would have had more trouble getting a job as a waiter in a restaurant than I did getting hired as a director!

EVERYBODY SAYS NO TO ME

Animation is good training for filmmaking, in the sense that you have to do everything yourself. You have to frame, you have to design the light, you have to act, you have to edit . . . it's very complete. Also, I think animation has given me a particular approach to filmmaking. It has probably given my films more originality in terms of tone and atmosphere.

The reason I prefer live action, though, is that animation is a very interior and very lonely occupation. I'm a fairly noncommunicative person, and when I work by myself, I find that the work has a tendency to feed into a negative side of my personality and that the ideas I get are a little too dark. The great thing about filmmaking is that it's a team enterprise. In fact, what surprised me the most the first time I made a film—besides the fact that you have to get up so early!—was the number of people involved in the process. That creates a real necessity to communicate, and the director's job often becomes more political than artistic, really, because you spend your time trying to convince all these people that your ideas are valid. I'm always amazed, on any given day, by how many times I hear the word "no" on a film set. "No, you can't do that. No, you can't have this. No, no, no . . ." It's a real human and strategic challenge to get things done your way. I mean, if I want actors to do something, I can't possibly go to them and say, "Do that!" I have to explain why, I have to convince them it's a good idea.

And it's the same with studio executives. I can't afford to go to war with them. It's too dangerous and, I find, much too exhausting. I admire the integrity of some people who fight with the studios over everything, but I think that in the end, it's more destructive than anything else. Because either the films don't get made, or they get made under such pressure and tension that the result inevitably suffers. I think you have to find a way to maneuver through the problems, and sometimes it may mean saying yes to something and hoping that the studio won't remember and that you'll be able to do it the way you wanted anyway. This may sound cowardly, but I think it's just a pragmatic survival technique. Of course, there are times when you *have* to fight. But the good director is the one who's able to determine which battles deserve to be fought and which are just a matter of ego.

IF I WROTE, IT WOULDN'T MAKE SENSE

I don't actually write, but I'm always involved in the writing process of my films. A director has to make the film his own; that's essential, and that has to happen before shooting. In the case of *Edward Scissorhands*, for instance, it is obvious that even though I didn't write the script myself, I "directed" the writing so much that, in the end, the material became mine more than the writer's. The reason I don't write is that if I did, I'm afraid I would get too interiorized and not have as detached a point of view on the material as I think a director should. The end result might turn out too personal, and it might not make sense to anybody else. When I make a film, my goal is to tell a story. And to accomplish that, I think I need to keep a certain distance. Which is why I don't quite agree when people look at the character in *Edward Scissorhands* and say, "Oh, it's you!" It's not me. I do have a lot in common with that character, but if I had been talking about myself, I never could have treated the film with objectivity.

In any case, I don't feel that I need to write to be the "author" of my work. I don't think anybody can see any of my films and not know immediately that it's mine. There are obvious clues, recurrent themes and ideas that you can notice here and there, usually in the backdrop of the story. Which is why I always loved the fairy-tale format, because it allows you to explore different ideas in a very symbolic manner, through imagery that is less literal, more sensorial. Rather than making images that explain things in a very concrete way, I like to make images that you can feel. I wasn't educated with ideas about strict narrative structure. Far from it. In fact, I grew up watching horror films, where the story really didn't matter but where the images were so heavy that they stayed with you and where, in a sense, these images *became* the story. And that's what I've tried to reproduce in my films.

YOU DON'T KNOW BEFORE YOU SHOOT

On a film set, and even more so on a Hollywood film set, the stakes are so high and the pressure is so huge that you want to plan as many things as you can in advance. But the more films I make, the more I realize that spontaneity is really the best approach, because—and that is definitely the biggest lesson I have drawn from my experience so far—you do not know anything until you actually get on the set. You can rehearse all you want, you can storyboard each shot if it reassures you, but once you get on the actual location, none of that means very much. Storyboards will always be less interesting than what reality offers because they're two-dimensional and the set is a tri-dimensional medium. So I tend not to rely on storyboards too much. They get in the way; people take them too literally. And it's the same with actors. They never behave the same when they're on the actual set, with costumes and make-up. So I try not to have any preconceived ideas anymore when I arrive on set. I leave a big part to the magic of the moment. And in a way, every film is an experiment in itself. Of course, the studios do not want to hear that. They want to believe that you know exactly what you're doing. But the truth is that the most important decisions on a film are made at the last moment and that chance is an important factor. It's the best way to work, and I would even go as far as to say that it's the only way to make an interesting film.

I LIKE WIDE LENSES

When I talk about working intuitively, I don't mean that you can do just about anything. In fact, it's very much the opposite, because you can improvise only if you have decided on a very strict set of parameters beforehand. Otherwise, you end up with chaos. The first thing you need to choose carefully is your team. You have to be sure that everybody is on the same wavelength, that they're all trying to make the same film, that they will understand everything you try.

After that, you need a certain methodology in the work process. Personally, I like to begin a scene by placing the actors on the set, so that I find the right relationship between the characters and the space around them. That's how I find the heart of the scene, how I determine whether it is being told from the point of view of one of the characters or from some exterior point of view.

Once I've found that, I send the actors to costume and make-up, and I work on the frame and the light with the director of photography. I have a fondness for very wide lenses, like the 21 millimeter (probably influenced by the wide frames used in animation), and so we always begin with that.* If it doesn't work, we slowly build our way toward longer lenses until we find something that works. But I never go beyond a 50 millimeter. And I use telephoto lenses only as a sort of punctuation. I use them in the middle of a scene the same way you would use a comma in the middle of a sentence.

In terms of camera placement, I go very much by instinct. When I shoot a dialogue scene, for instance, I don't do it in the traditional way—you know, master shot, then shot and reverse-shot on each actor. I try to find the most interesting shot for the scene and shoot it, and then I think about a couple of other shots that might match well with it in the editing. I never see very far ahead; I really move from one shot to the next. And I don't cover much. In fact, I really try not to shoot anything if I'm not sure that it will be in the final cut. First, because it is a waste of time, and time is something you

---

*In animation, frames are usually wide, with a great depth of field and a richness in the details. To obtain the same look in live action, one would have to shoot with a very wide-angle lens.

cannot afford to waste on a shoot. But also because, whether
you want to or not, you get emotionally attached to every
image you create. And if you shoot so much that after the first
cut, it becomes obvious you have to take an hour out of the
film, that can be painful. So the more rigorous you can
manage to be on the set, the less agony you will face during
editing.

USE WHAT'S INSIDE THE ACTOR

I never ask actors to audition because that's really pointless. I
don't need to know if an actor can act—he or she usually can.
What I need to know is whether he or she fits the part, and the
answer really has nothing to do with acting.

For instance, people often think that I work with Johnny
Depp because we're very similar. But the reason I originally
hired him on *Edward Scissorhands* was that at the time, he
was trapped inside an image that he had trouble dealing with.
He was the star of a teenage TV show, but he longed for
something completely different. And so he was perfect for the
role of Edward.

It's the same with Martin Landau in *Ed Wood*. I thought,
"Here's someone who started his career working with Hitchcock and ended up playing small parts in TV shows twenty
years later. He'll understand perfectly what Bela Lugosi went
through. He'll understand it on a human level without
overdramatizing the character." Also when I chose Michael
Keaton to play Batman, most people didn't understand. But
Michael has always fascinated me because he has a double-
edged personality, half-joking, half-psychotic. And I really
think you need to be a little schizophrenic like that to go running around in a Batman suit.

DIRECTING IS LISTENING

If you've done your casting well, then ninety percent of your job as an actors' director is done. But of course, the remaining ten percent is more complex because every actor is different; each one has his own way of working, of communicating. And you cannot guess what it's going to be like.

Take Jack Palance, for instance. Not exactly someone you would expect to be a tortured actor. Well, on the first shooting day of *Batman*, we were supposed to shoot a very basic scene where the gangster played by Jack steps out of the bathroom. He asks me, "How do you want me to do that?" and I answer, "Well, you know . . . it's a very basic shot: you just open the door and step out and walk toward the camera, that's it." So Jack goes behind the door, we roll the camera, and I say "Action!" but ten seconds go by and nothing happens. We cut, I call to Jack through the door: "Everything all right?" He says, "Yeah, yeah." Fine. We get the camera rolling again, and I say "Action!" and nothing happens. We cut; I call to Jack through the door and try to explain again: "It's just a shot where you come out of the bathroom, Jack. OK?" He answers "OK," we roll the camera again, and I say, "Action!" and once again, nothing. So we cut, and I decide to go see him, to ask what's the matter. And he gets very upset. I mean, he stares at me angrily and says, "Will you stop *pushing* me! Can't you see I need some time to concentrate!" I was just speechless. To me, it was just a stupid shot of someone getting out of a bathroom, but to him, there was obviously something much more complex going on.

That day, I understood how important it is to listen to actors. You have to direct them, of course, but all that really means is showing them what the objective is. After that, it's really up to them to decide *how* they want to reach that objective. The reason I like working with Johnny Depp, for instance, is that he will always try a different tone, from take to take, until we find something that works. I rehearse very little because I'm always scared that the acting might become too technical and that we will lose the magic that usually happens on the first takes. Also, I make it a point not to look at the scene on the video control but to watch the actors directly. Otherwise, I think it might create a distance between the actors and me and, ultimately, between the actors and the audience.

EVERYTHING SURPRISES ME—AND THEN AGAIN, NOTHING DOES

I never believe it when directors claim that their movies are exactly the way they imagined in their heads. It's impossible. There are just too many aspects you cannot control, every day, on a film set. At best, you can hope that the film will be in the same spirit as what you had in mind. But the final result will always be a surprise. And I think that's what makes it so magical. On the other hand, I tend to subscribe to the idea that, in a sense, you're always making the same film over and over again. You are who you are; your personality is usually the consequence of what you went through during your childhood, and you spend your life, consciously or not, rehashing the same ideas over and over again. It's true of all human beings, and it's even more true of artists. Whatever subject you tackle, you always end up taking a different approach with the same obsessions. In a way, it's annoying, because you'd like to think you're evolving. But at the same time, it's exciting, because it's like a never-ending challenge. It's like a curse you're desperately trying to break.

Films: *Pee-Wee's Big Adventure* (1985), *Beetlejuice* (1988), *Batman* (1989), *Edward Scissorhands* (1990), *Batman Returns* (1992), *Ed Wood* (1994), *Mars Attacks!* (1996), *Sleepy Hollow* (1999), *Planet of the Apes* (2001)

DAVID CRONENBERG
b. 1943, Toronto, Canada

David Cronenberg's films are, to say the least, disturbing. They usually center around the worst things that can happen to the human body, from broken bones to decaying flesh. Ever since Videodrome, *when the actor James Woods extracted a video-tape from his own entrails, the director's obsession with this subject matter has made for films both repulsive and fascinating, such as the brilliant* Dead Ringers, *probably his most accessible film, and* Crash, *which some people find unbearable to watch.*

I expected to meet a tortured, somewhat intimidating person, someone who would either laugh at my questions or answer in a language so personal that I would understand very little. But David Cronenberg is exactly the opposite of the stereotype of the eccentric, introverted director—at least on the surface. Calm, warm, elegant, articulate, he is someone with whom you instantly feel comfortable. If you didn't know he was a filmmaker, you would probably guess he was a professor of literature at an Ivy League college—a professor, however, endowed with a much more provocative mind than any of his students.

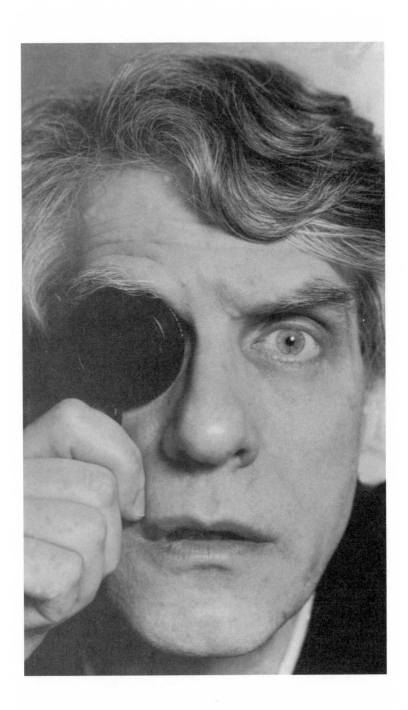

▨ Master Class with David Cronenberg

I became a director by accident. I always thought I would be a writer, like my father. I liked movies, as an audience member, but I never imagined that one could actually make a career in filmmaking. I lived in Canada and movies came from Holly-wood, which was not only in another country—it was in a dif-ferent world! When I was around twenty, however, something strange happened. A friend of mine from university had been hired to play a small part in a feature, and to see someone that I knew in everyday life on a movie screen was something of a shock. It might seem ridiculous today, when ten-year-old chil-dren are making movies with their video camcorders, but at the time, it was like an epiphany for me. I started thinking, "Hey, you could do that too . . ."

At that point, I decided to write a screenplay. But of course I had no practical knowledge of how to write for films. So I did the most logical thing: I picked up an encyclopedia and tried to learn film technique from it. Needless to say, the information it gave me was a little too basic. So I bought film magazines, figuring I would learn more. But I couldn't understand a word I read. The technical slang was just unde-cipherable for a novice like me.

What I liked about the magazines, however, were the pic-tures taken on film sets, particularly those showing filmmak-ing equipment. I have always been fascinated by machinery; it's something I really have a feel for. I can take anything apart, put it back together, and in the process understand how it works. So I figured the best way to learn was to actually use the equipment. I went to a camera rental company and be-came friends with the owner, who let me toy around with the cameras, the lights, the tape recorders . . . Sometimes, cam-eramen would come to pick up their equipment and would give me tips on lighting, lenses, and so on. And finally, one day, I decided to have a go at it. I rented one of the cameras and made a small short film. And another. And another. But I still considered it a hobby; I wasn't seriously thinking of directing films until I wrote a script that a production company wanted to buy. Suddenly, I realized that the idea of someone else making that film was unbearable, and I refused to sell the script unless they let me direct the movie. We fought for more than three years, but I eventually won, and this film launched my career as a director.

A FILMMAKER MUST KNOW HOW TO WRITE

As I said earlier, I always thought that my "serious" career would be as a writer, and for that reason, I think, I still consider literature a "higher" art form than film. Surprisingly, though, when I once talked about it with Salman Rushdie, whom I consider to be one of the most interesting writers of his generation, he looked at me as though I were a madman. He thought exactly the opposite. Having grown up in India, where film is highly regarded, he told me that he would give anything for the opportunity to make a film someday. It turned into a complex debate; I gave him examples of things he had written that could never be properly transcribed in images, and he gave me examples of films that no books could ever compete with. We eventually agreed that today, film and literature not only feed on one another but also complete each other. You cannot compare them anymore.

However, I do think there is a big difference between directors who write and directors who don't. I strongly believe that in order to be a complete filmmaker, you have to write your own scripts. In the past, I even argued that the filmmaker had to be the author of the *original idea* that the film was based on. But then I made *The Dead Zone,* which was adapted from a Stephen King novel, and lost a little of that arrogance.

THE LANGUAGE OF A FILM DEPENDS ON ITS AUDIENCE

Filmmaking is a language, and no language can exist without grammar. It's the basis of all communication: everybody agrees that certain signs mean certain things. However, inside that language, there is a real flexibility. And your job, as a filmmaker, is to find, for every shot, the right balance between what's expected, what's necessary, and what's exciting. You can use a close-up shot in a conventional way—to draw attention to something—or you can use it exactly for the opposite, as diversion.

If you play around with film language, the result is bound to be a little more dense, a little more complex, and the viewing experience should be a little richer for the audience. However, that implies that your audience already has a certain knowledge of film language. Otherwise, they will feel lost and eventually give up on your film. In other words, in order to communicate intensely with a hundred people, you might lose a thousand on the way. When Joyce wrote *Ulysses,* for instance, it was a rather experimental book, but most people were able to follow. But after that, he wrote *Finnegans Wake* and lost a lot of readers because in order to understand this book, you almost had to learn a new language, and very few people are willing to make that kind of effort. So it really is up to you, as a filmmaker, to decide how far you want to go, depending on how large an audience you wish to reach. Oliver Stone once asked me whether I was content to be a marginal filmmaker. I understood what he meant; there was nothing condescending in his question. He knows that I could be making mainstream films if I wanted to. And I answered that I was happy with the

size of my audience. But I think this is something that a director must somehow be able to determine in advance—what
kind of an audience he wants to have—because it will necessarily influence the language that he will be able to use.

A THREE-DIMENSIONAL MEDIUM

I remember that the first time I found myself on a film set,
what frightened me the most was the notion of space, because
I was used to writing, which is a two-dimensional medium,
and I discovered that film was a three-dimensional one. I'm
not talking about the visual aspect of film, of course. I mean
the set itself. It's an environment where you not only have to
deal with space but also with people and objects that have a
relationship with that space. And not only do you have to organize all these elements as efficiently as possible, but you
have to do it in a way that eventually makes sense. It might
sound abstract when I say it, but believe me, when you're
dealing with it, it's extremely concrete. Because the camera
has a place of its own within that space. It's like another actor.
And in a lot of first films, I notice the same problem over and
over again: the inability to make the camera "dance," to properly organize the sort of gigantic ballet that a film set inevitably turns into.

On the other hand, the wonderful thing is that most decisions come in a totally instinctive manner. Once again, when
I made my first film, I wasn't sure whether or not I would be
able to direct images, because I had never studied visual arts. I
had no idea whether or not I would be able to do something
as basic as decide where to set the camera for a given shot. I
had nightmares in which I realized I had no opinion on the
matter. But when I got onto the set, I discovered it was a totally visceral thing. I mean, I would sometimes look into the

camera's viewfinder and get physically sick because I didn't like the frame. I wasn't quite able to explain exactly why, but I knew it had to be changed. My instinct was telling me it wasn't right. Today, I still rely mostly on instinct.

The danger of that, of course, is that the more experienced you get, the easier it is to fall into a sort of routine. You know what works; you know what's efficient, what's comfortable. You end up directing the whole film on autopilot and leave no room for innovation, for surprises. So you have to remain alert. In any case, I am not one of these directors that are obsessed with the camera. It is not my priority when I arrive on the set. I prefer to work with the actors first, as if I were making a stage play, and then I figure out a way to shoot it with the camera. I approach it as though I were making a documentary of what I rehearsed with the actors. Of course, some scenes are purely visual, and in that case I start with the camera. But most of the time, my main concern remains the dramatic essence of the scene, and I don't want anything to interfere with that.

ONE FILM, ONE LENS

The more films I make, the more minimalist my approach becomes, to the point where I sometimes shoot an entire film with the same lens—in the case of *eXistenZ*, a 27-millimeter lens. I have a desire to be both direct and simple, like Robert Bresson when he started shooting everything with a 50-millimeter lens. That's the complete opposite of a Brian De Palma, for instance, who is always looking for a greater visual complexity, always trying to manipulate the image a little more. I'm not criticizing what he does—in fact, I completely understand it on an intellectual level. He just has a different approach, that's all.

One tool I never use is the zoom lens because it doesn't correspond to my idea of filmmaking. The zoom is just an optical gadget; it's purely practical. And I will always prefer moving the camera, because I find that it physically projects you inside the film's space. And zooming doesn't achieve that. It keeps you outside.

ACTORS HAVE THEIR OWN REALITY

Most directors today come from a visual background, and so, when they make their first film, their biggest fear tends to be working with actors, the same way some directors used to come from the stage and were terrified at the idea of working with a camera. As for directors who come from writing, like me, well, that's even worse: they are used to working alone in a room, and now they have to deal with all that chaos! In any case, when it comes to working with actors, I think the main thing is to understand that the reality of an actor is different from that of a director.

At the beginning, I saw actors as enemies because I felt they didn't understand the pressure I was under. I was worried about trying to make the film in time and within budget, and all they seemed to be worried about was their hair, their make-up, and their costume. These things seemed totally trivial to me, of course. But in time, I understood I was wrong. These are their tools, and they're as important to them as the camera and the lights are to me. For a director, it's all about the film. But for an actor, it's all about the character. So they're not quite on the same wavelength, they're not quite in the same reality, but if the actors and the director communicate, they can move in the same direction together. Most young directors will try to bypass that problem by lying to the actors. I know this can happen—I've done it. But in time, I've come to realize that if you're honest, actors will not only be happy to help you solve your problems—they will make a point of it. Unless, of course, you run into crazy or out-of-control actors. I can tell you from personal experience, there are some. And in that case, all you can really do is pray.

I DON'T WANT TO KNOW WHY I MAKE FILMS

There is a scene in *eXistenZ* where Jennifer Jason Leigh says, "You have to play the game to know what the game is about." Clearly, that is how I regard filmmaking. I will never be able to explain what draws me toward a particular project, and it is only by making the film that I can understand why I'm making it, and why I'm making it that way. Most of my films are therefore a complete surprise when I see them finished. And this is not something that bothers me. In fact, it's something I look forward to. Some directors say that they have a very concrete vision of the film in their head before they make it, that if they projected the film they had in their mind it would be a ninety percent match with the actual finished product. I don't see how that could be, because there are too many small changes that occur, day after day, when you're making a film. Little changes that eventually add up to make a big difference from what you originally had in mind.

I know that Alfred Hitchcock claimed he was able to pre-visualize his films shot by shot. But I don't believe him. I think it was just his oversized ego talking. I think the most important thing is to be able to know, intuitively, that the decisions you're taking are the right ones, without trying to explain them rationally—at least not while you're making the film. You'll have plenty of time to analyze it once the film is finished. In fact, if what Hitchcock said was true, then I almost pity him. Because can you imagine spending one year of your life working on a film that you've already seen in your head? That would be the most boring thing!

Films: *Stereo* (1969), *Crimes of the Future* (1970), *Shivers (They Came from Within)* (1976), *Rabid* (1977), *The Brood* (1979), *Fast Company* (1979), *Scanners* (1981), *Videodrome* (1983), *The Dead Zone* (1983), *The Fly* (1986), *Dead Ringers* (1988), *Naked Lunch* (1991), *M. Butterfly* (1993), *Crash* (1996), *eXistenZ* (1999)

JEAN-PIERRE JEUNET
b. 1955, Roanne, France

A *few weeks before I wrote these lines, Jean-Pierre Jeunet released his fourth film,* Amélie (Le fabuleux destin d'Amélie
Poulain), *which became an enormous hit with French audiences. Huge crowds of spectators, from teenagers to senior citi-
zens, rushed to see—or see again—a film in which the director
has achieved a poetic mix of everyday life and magic. Since the
release of* Delicatessen, *Jeunet's visual talent has been indis-
putable, and his taste for slightly surreal humor was a breath of
fresh air for French cinema (as well as for Hollywood, to which
he brought his touch to the* Alien *series). But with* Amélie, *he
added a personal layer to the film that took him to a new level,
from excellent to magnificent.*

*To some extent, Jean-Pierre Jeunet is very similar to his films:
deeply rooted in the everyday life of France. You could easily
picture him as a café owner in a small village, but one with an
amazing interior life. He talks plainly and directly and knows
how to explain methods and techniques in minute detail. When
we met for this interview, he confided to me that after reading
David Lynch's master class, he had tried out Lynch's secret
method for the dolly move . . . and failed.* *

*See the Lynch interview, pages 125–132.

■ Master Class with Jean-Pierre Jeunet

No one has ever asked me to teach film. In ten years, I have been invited only twice to the FEMIS [the main French film school], and only to talk about sets or storyboards. It's too bad. I wouldn't mind trying it one day. The idea, of course, is not to tell students, "You have to do it this way," but to tell them, "Here's the way I do it."

When Wenders made *The State of Things* and wrote the following day's scenes each evening, that's the very opposite of Scorsese, who storyboards each shot of his film before shooting a take. However, in both cases, the end result is fantastic. Therefore, there is no general rule. Every approach is good as long as the film works. Each director has to find his or her own formula.

For instance, I personally never studied cinema in the classic sense. I come from a fairly modest background, where studying at a film school was out of the question. Therefore, I discovered it all by doing things instinctively. I started at the age of twelve with a View-Master, a machine that allows you to view three-dimensional images. I'd record sound effects, dialogue, and music that would give a dramatic tone to these sequences of banal images when they were played at the same time. After that, I turned to animation, which was a huge step toward filmmaking.

But let me digress for just a moment. There are three films that I saw in my youth that made a great impression on me. The first was Sergio Leone's *Once Upon a Time in the West*. I saw it when I was a teenager, and I was unable to speak for three days afterwards. With that film, I discovered that film could have a playful side. Even now, I'm unable to shoot a tracking shot without wondering how Leone would have done it. The second film was Stanley Kubrick's *A Clockwork Orange*. I saw it fourteen times on the big screen during its first run. It helped me understand the importance of visual aesthetics in film. As for the third film, it was a short animated film by Piotr Ramler that I came across by chance on TV when I was seventeen. I was immediately fascinated by the incredible potential of animation.

And that is why I started making short animated films with puppets, in collaboration with Marc Caro back then.* I think animation taught me the most about directing films, because when you work in animation, you control everything and do everything yourself: costumes, sets, lighting, framing, and even, in a way, actor direction. I would advise any future filmmaker to take a stab at animation because it's an excellent opportunity to make a whole film on your own. You learn to take an interest in every aspect of a film's production. It's a totally comprehensive style of training.

CREATING THE FILM, OR MAKING IT YOUR OWN

You make a film for yourself. That is an absolute necessity. You have to make it for the very first audience, yourself, because if you're not pleased with it, no one else will be. People often talk about "formula" filmmaking, but the only formula that I know is sincerity—and it's not a risk-free formula. But if you don't apply it, failure is guaranteed. When you make something that you like and audiences reject it, the experience can be painful. But I have discovered, especially through a number of commercials I've made, that when you make something that you yourself aren't exactly satisfied with and someone tells you it's great, that's even more painful and frustrating.

I think you need to put as much of yourself as you can into

---

*Marc Caro is the artist with whom Jean-Pierre Jeunet co-directed his first two films, *Delicatessen* and *The City of Lost Children* (*La cité des enfants perdus*).

each film. That's why, for a long time, I felt that it was impossible to shoot a film from a screenplay that I hadn't written myself. One of the main lessons I learned while working on *Alien Resurrection* is that [shooting a film you haven't written] actually makes things much easier. Because writing is laborious. It's an enormous emotional investment, and you find it hard to look objectively at what you're doing. However, when a screenplay turns up, it's very easy to see right away how you can improve on it. Then you simply have to find a way to make it your own.

My guideline on *Alien Resurrection* was that there should be one of my ideas in every scene. That was the way of making the film mine. True, I put in only small things, details, even. But, in the end, there's no doubt about it, my fingerprints are all over the film. Actually, one of the greatest compliments I got on the film was from fellow director Mathieu Kassovitz, who said, "It looks like a Jean-Pierre Jeunet film . . . with aliens in it." I think that a film for which you don't write the screenplay is a bit like an adopted child, whereas one that you write yourself is your own child. And after an experience like *Alien Resurrection*, I needed to get back to writing and to work on my *Amélie*.

A STORYBOARD ISN'T THERE TO BE RESPECTED

There is necessarily a basic grammar where directing is concerned. If you try to cheat with certain rules, the film no longer works. However, I think that the goal every director is aiming for is to break these rules, to use them or twist them to make something new, to discover something that has never been done before. Innovation is enormously satisfying. That's what moves me when I see a film. And it's from this angle that I think special effects can contribute something to a director's work. I know that the French tend to have a negative attitude toward special effects, thinking that they should be reserved for fantasy films. But that's a mistake. Special effects are not only used to show spaceships or drooling monsters—they also help push back the limits of possibility. And we should use them to renew film writing.

Robert Zemeckis is perfectly aware of this. In *Forrest Gump*, he uses special effects to allow his characters to meet President Kennedy or to fill a Washington park with people without spending a fortune on extras. I think that people show the same stupid reluctance toward special effects as they did toward sound when it first made its appearance in the late twenties. Effects are just another tool and nothing to be scared of—far from it. Directors should learn to approach them, saying, "What can I do with this without necessarily making the kind of film that I don't want to make?"

Another thing that French directors have a fairly negative attitude about is the storyboard. Personally, I lay out the whole film on storyboards because my work is very visual and requires a great deal of preparation. If you have a visual idea on the set, it's too late. At the same time, I'm the first to say that a storyboard isn't made to be respected but to be transcended. If an actor finds a brilliant idea or if you think of a way of shooting the same thing differently and better, then you have to change everything, no doubt about it. In other words, the storyboard is like a highway: you can turn off it from time to time to follow prettier country roads, but if you lose your way, you can always return to the highway. If you decide to follow country roads from the outset, there's a fair chance you'll lose your way and get bogged down.

When I shot the scene in *Delicatessen* where Marie-Laure Dougnac invites Dominique Pinon for tea, we rehearsed the scene dozens and dozens of times. And then, at the last minute, just before shooting it, I took Pinon to one side and said, "You're going to sit on her chair." As a result, Dougnac was thrown off balance, and the confusion she was supposed to show in the scene was totally realistic. When this kind of thing happens, it's magical. But I think that it's possible only if you improvise from something that has been well prepared in advance; otherwise, it becomes ridiculous.

I NEED TO FRAME BEFORE I CAN DIRECT

My desire is, above all, to create a graphic form of cinema. That's why I insist on framing each shot myself. I don't actually operate the camera, but I decide on the frame. To do that, I usually arrive on the set in the morning and use a camcorder with a freeze-frame function. I ask trainees to take the place of the actors. (The great thing in Hollywood is that every actor has a stand-in for this purpose.) Then I shoot my images and print them out onto photographic paper. When the rest of the crew members arrive, they see the "prefilmed" scene and know exactly what they have to do. Then I usually ask the actors to adapt to the frame that I have determined. In a comedy, this process is a little less strict. Generally, I get the actors to perform first to see what they're going to do, because if someone has a brilliant idea which requires him to move ten feet to the left, I'm clearly not going to prevent him from doing that.

I love the idea of being able to summarize a whole scene in one frame, whatever the graphic nature of the frame that brings the scene to life. It's for this reason that I use virtually only short lenses. I could shoot a whole film using just 18-millimeter and 25-millimeter lenses. In *Alien Resurrection*, I also used a 14-millimeter lens a great deal to make the sets more imposing. Using a wide-angle lens like that allows you to have a better-composed image, from a graphic point of view. But at the same time, its use requires a great deal of rigor or the film can seem tacky as soon as you move the camera. I also use long focal lengths at times, but only the very, very long ones. I don't use them too much because they're not a stylistic device but rather a practical one. By alternating very short and very long focal lengths, you give an impression of greater visual richness. It's a process that the American cinema has used a great deal in recent years but one that I feel goes against the notion of visual style. I used it a little in *Alien Resurrection* because it was a way of entering the Hollywood game. But on films like *Delicatessen* or *The City of Lost Children*, I have always avoided it.

Similarly, I never cover a scene. I don't shoot the same scene from three different angles. I make a choice and stick to it. Directors often say, "There aren't two ways to shoot a scene; there's only one, and it's the best." That's a little pretentious, but it's true. And there's nothing more intoxicating than allowing yourself no exit, trapping yourself and then arriving in the cutting room and realizing that it works. In fact, that attitude helped me a great deal on *Alien Resurrection*. Often, during editing, the studio would say to me, "Couldn't we try that differently?" and I'd answer, "No, sorry, I haven't shot anything else." There are camera movements that I loved but that the producers wanted to cut, but they weren't able to because I hadn't covered the scene from other angles and they were trapped. This, of course, requires an amazing amount of self-confidence. You can always fall into your own trap. Once again, that's why I prepare as many things as possible in advance.

THE BEAUTY OF A TRACKING SHOT COMES FROM ITS RIGOR

I'm very strict about camera movements: I feel that they must be regular and steady. During a tracking shot, I refuse to have the camera swivel or start moving to seek out details. When I see a cameraman touch the cranks during a tracking shot, I rap his fingers. I insist on total rigor since I believe that it lends elegance and power to the camera movement.

Moreover, this is what frustrated me about the Steadicam for many years: I felt that it was unable to attain such consistency. At the same time, it's an amazing tool that allows you to do things that would be impossible otherwise. And I've finally managed to find a Steadicam operator who is so strong that he manages to film the way I like — in other words, with a steadiness similar to that of a tracking shot on rails.

But apart from that, my mania is the entrance into the frame from below: the camera moves down and allows the character to enter the frame through the foot of it. I use this technique in an abstract manner, but it makes the characters' arrival incredibly dynamic. They do not appear, stepping into the frame, nor does the camera go looking for them. They pop up from below like a jack-in-the-box.

These entrances from the bottom or the back of the shot are also a direct influence from Sergio Leone. I remember a scene in *The Good, the Bad and the Ugly* in which Eli Wallach is leaning over a grave and, all of a sudden, a shovel lands next to him. Then the camera pulls back and we discover Clint Eastwood's boots. I often use that idea. For instance, in *Delicatessen*, when the old lady's ball of wool rolls over the ground, the camera pulls back at the same time and we discover the butcher's feet. This kind of movement, done at ground level and with a very short focal length, is very impressive.

THE DIRECTOR HAS TO YIELD TO THE ACTORS

If there's one thing that you can't learn, it's how to direct an actor. Directing consists of communicating your desires to the other person, and I think that each director has to find his or her own way of doing this. But the basic thing is to love doing it.

I remember that my major concern before *Delicatessen*, since I had mainly shot commercials until then, was how to confront the actors; I didn't know if I would be capable of directing them. But as soon as I started doing it, I enjoyed it. I could feel my veins physically filling with warmth. And once you enjoy doing this, you can only do it well. Therefore, you have to love doing it.

I also think that the casting process is very important. It's often said that ninety percent of the director's work occurs at the casting stage, and that's true. You mustn't hesitate about seeing a lot of people. But there, too, that implies that you know what you're looking for, because otherwise everything is open to confusion. However, if you have the character firmly in mind, the actors file past, and all of a sudden, the character is there in front of you. And that is an amazing feeling. Three seconds into her audition, I knew that Audrey Tatou was the Amélie I had been looking for, and I had to hide behind the camera so she wouldn't see my tears of joy.

Once you've chosen your actor, you simply have to direct him, which doesn't mean changing his performance style. The greatest mistake that a young director can make is to want to show the actor what to do. It's like asking an artist to design a poster but sketching it for him. An actor is a *performer*. He performs your words. It's true that sometimes you have a very precise idea of what you want. You want to demonstrate it, but you have to do everything you can to avoid doing so. Otherwise, you're likely to frustrate and terrify the actor.

No two actors are alike, and the director has to adapt to them, not the opposite. At times, when a director attains a certain status, actors tend to try to adapt to the director's technique, but I think that's a mistake. Some actors need to talk about their part for hours, but others, taking the opposite approach, prefer to work in a more instinctive manner. Jean-Claude Dreyfus, for example, hates rehearsing. You have to respect that. You have to understand how actors work and try to go toward them.

Personally, I like to rehearse a little or at least do a read-through, to know what the actor's going to do. But I cannot understand directors who create a whole psychodrama in order to "condition" their actors for the part. I find that unprofessional. Of all the actors I've met, Americans are clearly the ones who needed the least direction. Maybe because they are used to working with directors who stay behind their video monitor, fifty yards from the set.

OVERSIGHTS, ERRORS, DANGERS . . .

Just before I started shooting *Alien Resurrection*, I saw *The City of Lost Children* again in a Los Angeles theater. I was dismayed, as I am each time I view my work after a film is finished: I see only the mistakes. One of the things that struck me was how unclearly the story came across. And that would be my first warning to young directors. This kind of problem often arises from the pressure that reigns on a set and that occasionally prevents the director from thinking of small but vital details. After seeing *City* again, I made myself a list of ten commandments that I won't give here because I'd sound like a moron. They are such obvious things as always shooting a general establishing shot—basic things like that. But I stuck this list to my storyboard for *Alien Resurrection*, and I was amazed to see how often on the set I was forgetting all these obvious rules. Therefore, you have to be careful of that. You also should never hesitate to let people read a script's first draft or see a film's first cut. Because if you see that five out of ten people do not understand something, then it means you clearly have a problem.

The other main warning that I could give directors concerns the film's coherence. That's something impalpable and indescribable but that must come across. Sometimes you may want to make a special camera movement, or you may be offered a brilliant costume for one of the characters. But if it isn't consistent with the film as a whole, you have to do without it. That's not always easy.

Finally, the greatest difficulty and greatest danger for a director is adhering too tightly to the schedule. On the one hand, you can be tempted to cut or simplify things to adhere to the schedule and pacify the producers. But you risk paying a heavy price for this during editing if you're not satisfied with what you've shot. On the other hand, you must be able to make compromises at the right time. If you systematically oppose the producers, you end up having your own crew turn against you, and then you're heading straight for disaster. Therefore, you need to know when to bend and when to stand up to everyone.

Films: *Delicatessen* (1991), *The City of Lost Children* (*La cité des enfants perdus*) (1995), *Alien Resurrection* (1997), *Amélie* (*Le fabuleux destin d' Amélie Poulain*) (2001)

DAVID LYNCH
b. 1946, Missoula, Montana

David Lynch is not at all what you'd expect. The films he makes are usually strange and twisted, filled with ambiguous and sometimes frightening characters. But the man behind the camera is one of the plainest, warmest, and most charming directors I've ever met, which makes me even more worried about what truly goes on in the darker reaches of his mind!

I was only sixteen when I saw Eraserhead *for the first time. I had to leave the theater halfway through it because the experience made me too uneasy. It was as though someone had opened the door to a dark, creepy place that seemed both unreal and much too close for comfort. With time, this is exactly what I—and other fans—have come to love about Lynch's films: the way he manages to show us what lies beneath the surface, like the swarming bugs below the grass in the opening of* Blue Velvet *or that incredibly frightening dark hallway in* Lost Highway, *the film for which I went to interview Lynch in Los Angeles. He received me in a beautiful modern house near Mulholland Drive. On the terrace, several of his own in-progress paintings lay about. Lynch answered my questions good-naturedly, like a wise old man listening to a kid asking him about life. And when the interview was finally over, he smiled and asked me, "So? What do you think? Do I get the job?"*

▨ Master Class with David Lynch

I have never been asked to teach filmmaking, and I don't think I would be very good at it anyway. I took only one film course in my life, with a teacher named Frank Daniel. It was a course in film analysis, where he would ask students to watch films and to concentrate on one specific element at a time: picture, sound, music, acting . . . Afterwards, everyone in the class would compare notes, and the things we discovered were pretty amazing. It was a fascinating course, but what really made it work was that Daniel, like all great teachers, had the ability to inspire and to stimulate students.

I don't think I have that ability. I don't have an encyclopedic knowledge of film history, and I'm not very good at giving lectures, either, so I don't know what I could tell students, except to pick up a camera and go make a movie. After all, this is the way *I* learned. I originally wanted to be a painter. But while I was studying fine arts, I made a short animated film which I then projected, as a loop, on a sculpted screen. It was an experimental project; the idea was to make it look as though the painting was alive. A man saw it, liked it very much, and offered to pay me to make another one for him. I tried, but somehow I couldn't manage, and he said, "Never mind. Keep the money and do whatever you want." So I made a short film, which got me an award and financing to do *Eraserhead*. And that is how I got started.

MY REFERENCES

If I had to choose films that represent, for me, examples of perfect filmmaking, I think I could narrow it down to four.

The first would be 8½, for the way Federico Fellini managed to accomplish with film what mostly abstract painters do—namely, to communicate an emotion without ever saying or showing anything in a direct manner, without ever explaining anything, just by a sort of sheer magic. For similar reasons, I would also show *Sunset Boulevard*. Even though Billy Wilder's style is very different from Fellini's, he manages to accomplish pretty much the same abstract atmosphere, less by magic than through all sorts of stylistic and technical tricks. The Hollywood he describes in this film probably never existed, but he makes us believe it did, and he immerses us in it, like in a dream. After that, I would show *Monsieur Hulot's Holiday* for the amazing point of view that Jacques Tati casts at society through it. When you watch his films, you realize how much he knew about—and loved—human nature, and it can only be an inspiration to do the same. And finally, I would show *Rear Window*, for the brilliant way in which Alfred Hitchcock manages to create—or rather, re-create—a whole world within confined parameters. James Stewart never leaves his wheelchair during the film, and yet, through his point of view, we follow a very complex murder scheme. In the film, Hitchcock manages to take something huge and condense it into something really small. And he achieves that through a complete control of filmmaking technique.

STAY FAITHFUL TO THE ORIGINAL IDEA

At the beginning of every film, there is an idea. It may come at any time, from any source. It may come from watching people in the street or from thinking alone in your office. It make take years to come, too. I have known such dry periods, and who knows, it may take another five years until I get another idea I like for a film. What you need is to find that original idea, that spark. And once you have that, it's like fishing: you use that idea as bait, and it attracts everything else. But as a director, your main priority is to remain faithful to that original idea.

You will encounter many obstacles, and time can erase a lot of things in your mind. But a film is not finished until there is not one more shot to be edited, one more sound to be mixed. Every decision matters, however small. And every element can either make you move a little forward or a little backwards. You have to be open to new ideas, but at the same time, you must always stay focused on your original intention. It is a sort of standard against which you can test the validity of every new suggestion.

THE NEED TO EXPERIMENT

A director needs to think with both his brain and his heart. He has to constantly associate both intellect and emotions in the decision-making process. Telling a story is essential. The kinds of stories I like are those that contain a certain share of abstraction, that rely more on intuitive comprehension than logic. To me, the power of film goes beyond the simple task of telling a story. It has to do with the *way* you tell that story and how you manage to create a world of your own. Film has the power to depict invisible things. It works like a window through which you enter a different world, something close to a dream. I think film has that power because, unlike most other art forms, it uses time as part of its process. Music is a little bit like that, too. You start somewhere, and then, note by note, you slowly build up until you reach a particular note that creates a strong emotion. But it works only because of all the notes that came before, and the way they were orchestrated. The problem with that, of course, is that after a while, the basic rules cannot work as well. The element of surprise gets lost. And that is why I think it is essential to experiment. I have experimented on all my films, and sometimes I make mistakes. If I'm lucky, I realize in time, and change it before the film is finished. Otherwise, the mistake serves as a lesson for the next film. But sometimes, experimentation allows me to discover something wonderful which I couldn't have imagined or planned. And nothing else is as rewarding as that.

THE POWER OF SOUND

I discovered the power of sound right from the beginning. When I made that "live painting" with the projector and the sculpted screen, there was also the sound of a siren playing over it. Since then, I have always believed that sound is half of what makes a film work. You have the image on one side, the sound on another, and if you know how to combine them properly, then the whole is stronger than the sum of the parts.

The image is made up of different elements, most of them hard to control perfectly—light, frame, acting, and so on. Sound, however—and I include music in that category—is a concrete and powerful entity which physically inhabits the film. Of course, you have to find the right sound, which implies a lot of talking and a lot of tests. There are very few directors who are able to use sound beyond a purely functional aspect, and the reason for that is that they worry about sound only *after* the film is shot. Yet post-production schedules are usually so tight that they never have time to come up with anything interesting, either with the sound designer or the composer. That is why for the last few years—since *Blue Velvet*, I think—I have tried to do most of the music before the shoot. I discuss the story with my composer, Angelo Badalamenti, and records all sorts of music that I listen to as I'm shooting the film, either on headphones during dialogue scenes or on loudspeakers, so that the whole crew gets in the right mood. It's a great tool. It's like a compass helping you find the right direction.

I work the same way with songs. When I hear a song I like, I record it and store it somewhere until I find the right film in which to use it. For instance, there was a song by This Mortal Coil, "Song to the Siren," which I had always liked. I tried to use it on *Blue Velvet*, but it wasn't appropriate for the film. So I waited. And when I started to work on *Lost Highway*, I felt that this time, I could use it. There are lots of other songs which mean something to me and that I am waiting to use in one of my next films.

ACTORS ARE LIKE MUSICAL INSTRUMENTS

Finding an actor who can play a specific part is not that difficult. What's harder is finding the right one. What I mean is that, for any given part, there are six or seven actors who will probably give you a good performance. But they will all play something different. It's a little bit like music: you can play the same piece of music with a trumpet or a flute, and both will give you something wonderful, but in two different directions. And you have to decide what is the best choice.

Once you have chosen your actors, then I think the secret to getting the best performance is to create the most comfortable atmosphere you can on the set. You have to give the actors everything they need because, eventually, they're the ones making the biggest sacrifice. They're the ones standing in front of the camera. They're the ones who have the most to lose. And even though they might be enjoying themselves, they're still frightened about what the result will be like, and that is why they have to feel as safe as possible. I never try to trick or torture my actors. I never shout. Well, actually, I do, sometimes. But it's always out of frustration, never because I think it will help the scene. You have to talk a lot with the actors until you're sure that you're moving along the same track. And once everyone is attuned, then every word and every move the actors make will naturally turn out perfectly.

Rehearsals can help find the right tone. But you have to be

careful. Personally, I'm always worried about losing the spontaneity of the scene by rehearsing it too much; I don't want to
lose the magic that can sometimes happen on the first try. ·

ACCEPT YOUR OBSESSIONS

People don't like to repeat themselves, and no one likes to do
the same thing over and over again. At the same time, everyone is a little bit enslaved to his or her own particular tastes.
This is something you have to accept without necessarily
getting trapped by it. Every director evolves, but it's a slow
process, and there's no reason to try to rush it.

It's obvious that I like a certain type of story, a certain type
of character. There are details that come back in every one of
my films, like obsessions. For instance, I am fascinated by texture—I love that word—and it is something that plays a big
part in my films. But it's never a conscious decision. I always
realize it afterwards, never before. And I don't even think it's
worth thinking about because in the end, there's nothing you
can do about your obsessions. You can talk meaningfully only
about things that fascinate you. You can create stories or characters only if you're in love with them. It's like women: some
men only love blondes and, consciously or not, will never
have an affair with a brunette, until maybe one day they meet
a brunette who is so special that she changes everything. It's
the same with movies. The director's choices work on the
same obsessional level. And it's not something you must try to
avoid. On the contrary, you have to accept it and even maybe
explore it.

MY SECRET DOLLY MOVE

Every director has a few particular technical tricks. For instance, I like to play with contrasts; I like using lenses that give

a greater depth of field; and I like extreme close-ups, like the famous match shot in *Wild at Heart*. But none of this is systematic. However, I have a very particular way of getting the dolly to move. It is something I experimented with on *Eraserhead* and that I have always used since. The way it works is that you load the dolly with sandbags until it's so heavy that it feels like it's never going to move. It takes several men to push the dolly, and once it starts moving, it's very slow, like an old train engine. After a while, though, it gains so much momentum that the men who were pushing have to start pulling, to hold it back. They have to pull with all their might. It's exhausting, but the result on film is incredibly fluid and graceful.

I think the best camera move in all of my films is in a scene from *The Elephant Man*, when the character played by Anthony Hopkins discovers the Elephant Man for the first time and the camera moves close to see the reaction on his face. Technically speaking, the move was very good, but also, just when the camera stopped in front of Hopkins's face, he cried a tear. That wasn't planned at all, it's just one of those magic things that happen on movie sets. And even though it was the first take, when I saw that, I decided it was pointless to even try a second one.

STAY THE MASTER OF YOUR FILM

Since my films tend to either surprise or shock people, I am often asked if it's a mistake to try to please the audience. The fact is, I don't think it's a bad thing, as long as you don't go against your own pleasure and your own vision to do it. In any case, it's impossible to please everyone. Steven Spielberg is a very fortunate director because audiences happen to love his films, and it's obvious that he's happy making them. If you try to please audiences, but in order to accomplish that you make

a film that you might not want to see yourself, then you're
heading for a disaster. This is why I find it absurd for any self-
respecting director to make a film without control of the final
cut. There are too many decisions to make, and it is the director who has to make them—not a group of people who have
no emotional investment in the film.

So my advice to every young filmmaker is this: remain in
control of your film from beginning to end. It's better not to
make a film at all than to give up the power of final decision.
Because if you do, you will suffer immensely. And I know that
from experience. I shot *Dune* without final cut, and I was so
damaged by the result that it took me three years before I
could make another film. I still haven't gotten over it, even today. It's a wound that won't heal.

Films: *Eraserhead* (1978), *The Elephant Man* (1980), *Dune*
(1984), *Blue Velvet* (1986), *Wild at Heart* (1990), *Twin Peaks:
Fire Walk with Me* (1992), *Lumière et compagnie* (co-director)
(1995), *Lost Highway* (1997), *The Straight Story* (1999), *Mulholland Drive* (2001)

BIG GUNS

Oliver Stone
John Woo

As human beings, they are complete opposites. The first is a driven, flamboyant, and dizzying whirlwind of a man; the other is shy, sweet, and enigmatic. As directors, however, they have a very similar approach to cinema, making films of gigantic proportions while keeping them undeniably personal. How they manage to do this within the studio system is no doubt a constant source of bewilderment to—and admiration from—other filmmakers.

OLIVER STONE
b. 1946, New York City

No one will be surprised to learn that Oliver Stone is an intense man. We'd originally scheduled one hour for this interview but had to extend it to two because Stone couldn't help shifting gears with stories about Vietnam, divorce, politics, film critics, and the JFK conspiracy. He had so much to say, and so much energy, that I sometimes felt like a novice wrangler desperately trying to rein in a mustang. Yet there was something very humane about the whole thing.

The intensity is precisely what audiences love—or hate— about Oliver Stone's films. As with all artists who have a strong point of view, there is no middle ground with Stone. You either subscribe unconditionally or reject his work completely. And though he's certainly a very American filmmaker, there's also something quite European in Stone's approach to the process because he challenges the audience and forces them to pick sides. He is the only "political" director I can think of working in Hollywood today. Films such as Salvador, Platoon, JFK, Natural Born Killers, and even Wall Street were courageous choices when they were made. Though Stone's films have now become undisputed classics, there was something disturbing to the American public when each one was released. Maybe Oliver Stone's most recent films have become a trifle less aggressive, but the man is still boiling inside.

▧ Master Class with Oliver Stone

I've often thought about teaching filmmaking. The only reason I don't do it, I'm ashamed to confess, is the money. I would have to stop working for that, and I can't afford to. I guess maybe with the Internet, there might be new ways to do it, but then again, you can never substitute the real thing.

I remember that when I went to film school in New York, I had some very inspiring teachers, including Haig Manoogian and his star pupil, Martin Scorsese. They both had an amazing energy. However, the thing that probably had the biggest influence on my work as a director was going to the Vietnam War. I used to be a very cerebral person until I went there. I was mostly interested in writing. But in Vietnam, everything changed. First of all, I couldn't write—for very practical reasons, such as humidity. Yet I was surrounded by the most dramatic setting you can imagine, and I wanted to keep a record of it. So I bought a camera and started taking pictures. And little by little, I discovered the sensuality of the picture, which I found to be much stronger than the sensuality of anything written. I became more visceral than cerebral. And my concentration became sharper, too. The war gives you an approach of just watching the six inches in front of your face. Because when you walk in the jungle, you have to be very careful of what's in front of you. You intensify the six inches in front of your face, which, in a sense, is also what you do in a movie.

I didn't realize all of this when I was there, of course. It's only when I came back to New York and started making films that it became apparent. Actually, it's Scorsese who pointed it out. I had made three short films that were terrible, and Martin encouraged me to use my experience and talk about it. So I made a twelve-minute film called *Last Year in Vietnam*, which was about the clash between my war experiences and life in New York. And I remember that after I screened it, the other film students, who were very competitive and used to tear each other apart, became incredibly silent. That's when I understood that I had to fuel my movies with my own life, because that's what makes the best films.

The funny thing, though, is that this "personal" approach to filmmaking is much more accepted in Europe than it is in the United States. When Truffaut or Fellini made films about their own lives, people called it genius. But if you do it in this country, people call you an egomaniac. So you have to hide behind a lot of things.

A FILM IS A POINT OF VIEW; EVERYTHING ELSE IS JUST SCENERY

The most important thing a director needs is a point of view. When you see a movie, if you're alert, it's the thinking that went on behind the movie that's interesting, really. The rest is just . . . scenery. Even the script. In the first ten or fifteen shots of a film, you can usually tell whether the director's thinking and what he's thinking about. And yet, film is a collaborative art; it really is. On *Any Given Sunday*, for instance, I had so many shots to edit—thirty-seven hundred!—that I had six editors working. I also had several composers on the score.

Some people call it "corporate" art. But I dispute that. A movie is a collective effort, yes, but you have to have a person in charge, a person whose vision makes it all coherent. Otherwise, the collective won't add up. I have a point of view which, once again, is the result of my experience in Vietnam. All the things that I'm criticized for—my loudness, my intensity—they all come from the war. I keep being influenced by the beauty and the horror of everything that I saw over there. And in a way, all my films are war movies. Although that's probably the only link I would see between them.

If you look at most directors, they have a coherent body of work, with a couple of films that everyone agrees on. With me, it's always chaos. I notice that the people who love *The Doors* usually do not like *Wall Street*, that those who love *Platoon* hate *Natural Born Killers*, and so on. No one group is ever in agreement. That's a little disturbing. But I guess that's also good because it means I'm diversifying. And that is what you aim for as a director. In any case, I have my vision of things, and it's different from that of other directors—which doesn't mean it's better or worse.

For instance, when I wrote the script for *Scarface*, I had my own vision of it, and Brian De Palma did something different, which I found amazing. I had written a gangster film and he chose to shoot it like an opera. And so, scenes that I had written as thirty seconds long ended up lasting two minutes. There were a lot of excesses in all aspects of the film, but they were totally logical in terms of De Palma's vision, and I think that's what made it work so well in the end.

INDEPENDENCE IS A FAKE PROBLEM

People often ask me how I manage to work for big Hollywood studios and still keep my identity. But I don't get it. This whole debate of studios versus independents is just mythology, it's more of a sixties mentality of "us versus them."

Hollywood studios are essentially entities. They all operate in a form of chaos, and if you're smart and alert, you always know how to take advantage of that chaos when you make a film. I managed to make twelve movies—some of which were extremely political—inside the studio system, and I did them in a very independent manner. The studios may have their bad sides, but they also have one major thing going for them: their distribution network. And personally, when I make a movie, I like it to be seen by as many people as possible. I make films for an audience—although I guess I make them for myself first. I need to be pleased with what I do. And then I pray that I will reach a consensus with the audience.

The hardest thing, really, is to figure out who your audience is. Because it changes. Lately, I find that it has very much turned into a television-watching audience. I noticed a softening in American cinema over the last twenty years, and I think it's a direct influence of TV. I would even say that if you want to make movies today, you'd be better off studying television than film because that's the market. Television has diminished the audience's attention span. It's hard to make a slow, quiet film today. Not that I would ever want to make a slow, quiet film anyway!

THE SCRIPT IS NOT A BIBLE

Shooting is the critical part of the whole filmmaking process because anything can happen and you don't get a second chance. That is why, when I get on the set in the morning, I usually have a list of fifteen to twenty shots that I want to make that day, and I go for the money right away. I start with the most important because I never know what I'll have at the end of the day. I might have twenty-five shots, or I might have two. I usually have a picture in my mind of what the scenes should look like, but I also know that more often than not, I will end up modifying that vision, mostly because actors will bring last-minute ideas during the rehearsals. And I'm open to that. The script is not a bible to me. It's a process. I think it's dangerous to be too rigid about the script. Shooting has to be fluid.

So I always start by rehearsing with the actors. Ideally, we've already rehearsed that scene before we even go into production. And because the actors have a memory of it, it usually leads to something new, I find. In any case, it's better to be alone with them. That means you have to ask everybody else to leave the set. And sometimes it takes an hour, sometimes three. Sometimes you don't shoot your first shot of the day until after lunch. You have to wait until you have found the essence of the scene. And sometimes you have to improvise. I often shoot with several cameras; I used as many as seven when I was making *JFK*. And you can't write for seven cameras, so a lot will have to be improvised on the set. In the case of *JFK*, we shot just the assassination scene over and over again for two weeks until we felt we had enough material to play with in the editing.

EVERY ACTOR HAS HIS LIMITATIONS

I have the feeling that most young directors are afraid of actors. They come from film school with a heavy technical background, but they don't know how to deal with an actor. Some of them barely even talk to their actors. I am amazed to hear that some directors who make excellent films just put the actors in front of the camera and shoot. They don't talk, they don't rehearse. I don't know how they do it because, in my experience, actors will give you a good performance only if you force them to look into themselves and get out of their comfort zone. But that takes time and discussion. Actors like to do that because what they want, ultimately, is for people to see them in a way they've never been seen before. But they can't achieve that by themselves. They need guidance. It has to be a collective thing. As individuals, we're all selfish. And the best thing we can do as people is to help the other person be better. So as a director, you have to find the raw material, then take that person to a place he or she has never been before. And that's how you bring out the best in actors.

Of course, you have to cast the right actors to begin with. Because whatever they say, actors have their limitations, and they can't go beyond them. They can improve, they can stretch a little further, but they can never be someone they're not. I've never seen an actor do that. I mean, Laurence Olivier was trained for Shakespeare. Robert de Niro, as good as he is, has his range. You will never see him play a warm character. On the other hand, when I chose Woody Harrelson and Juliette Lewis for *Natural Born Killers*, for instance, most people were surprised. They felt it was an out-of-character choice. But I felt that, even though he had mainly played in comedies, Woody Harrelson had a lot of hidden anger in him. And in Juliette Lewis, I had sensed a very savage female energy. So that even though they did not get along in private, they had a great relationship on film.

The other important decision you have to deal with when casting is the question of the actor's "weight." Given the nature of the films I make, I usually need a strong actor in the lead to serve as an anchor. That's pretty much what Kevin Costner did in *JFK*. And then I wanted known faces as supporting cast because there is so much information to pass along that these faces help the audience along the way, as markers do on a road. The flip side of this, of course, is that it becomes very hard to get all these people to just stand around in the background all day. They feel underused.

I CONTROL NOTHING

One thing I never hear directors say is that when you make a film, you can easily be wrong about a lot of things. There are a lot of delusions. In a script, I sometimes read a scene that I think will be great, and then I put it on film and it doesn't work. Or the opposite. It's total chaos. No one will admit to it, but truthfully, there is that element. When I hear writers talking about successful films and saying, "It was all in the script, the movie already existed on paper," I think they're being, at best, totally naïve. It's more fluid than that. I used to say,

"Script is everything," because that was the way I had been trained. But today I think too much is made of the script.

Look at the studios, who invest so much time, money, and energy getting their scripts rewritten over and over again . . . what do they get in the end? Perfect scripts that turn into terrible movies. Because filmmaking doesn't work that way. It works in a magical way. For instance, when I read the script of *Pulp Fiction*, I thought it would never work, that it was too talky and incredibly self-indulgent. But then I saw the way Quentin Tarantino did it, and the actors he chose to do it, and it became totally different. There are things you just can't write, like the way an actor will look at another actor. And these little things are everything in a movie. So I think that as filmmakers, we don't truly have control over everything. And in the end, it can be the movie directing us rather than the opposite.

Films: *Seizure* (1974), *The Hand* (1981), *Salvador* (1986), *Platoon* (1986), *Wall Street* (1987), *Talk Radio* (1988), *Born on the Fourth of July* (1989), *The Doors* (1991), *JFK* (1991), *Heaven and Earth* (1993), *Natural Born Killers* (1994), *Nixon* (1995), *U-Turn* (1997), *Any Given Sunday* (1999)

JOHN WOO

b. 1946, Guangzhou, China

After a decade of dominating Hong Kong's box office with his action films, John Woo gained international recognition in 1989 with The Killer, a film in which he raised the action genre to an operatic level.

Like every successful foreign filmmaker, he was lured to Hollywood—and like many, he quickly realized the grass was not greener there. His first film for the studios, Hard Target, was apparently a less than enjoyable experience. "Too many meetings, too much politics," he says. The result was quite disappointing, too. But rather than go back to where he was revered, John Woo stayed in the United States and persisted. On his next film, Broken Arrow, he managed to get a little more control. Then, on the one that followed, Face/Off, he finally was able to show what he could really do with film.

Today, there is no question that John Woo is the greatest action-film director around, but he's much more than that. He's a true auteur whose work is suffused with strong personal values. The reason his films have had such an impact on audiences is that beyond their visual perfection and their technical innovation, they possess something most blockbusters usually lack: a soul. That's why it's not really so surprising that when you finally meet the man who has directed such notoriously violent films, he turns out to be a shy, self-effacing person who tells you with a wry smile that all he ever wanted was to write poetry.

▣ Master Class with John Woo

Ever since *The Killer*, I have often been asked to teach film-making. I have had offers in Hong Kong, of course, but also in Taiwan, in Berlin, and in America. But I always turned them down. Not because I don't believe film can be taught, but because I don't think I would be a good teacher. I am far too shy to do a lecture in front of a whole classroom.

What I do, however, whenever I travel to promote my films, is try to meet one or two students privately and have a talk with them. If they've already made films, we discuss technical things. Otherwise, we talk about movies, my three personal favorites being *Jules and Jim*, *Psycho*, and *8½*. I encourage them to go and see as many films as possible because that's the way I learned.

When I grew up in Hong Kong, there was no film school. And had there been one, I wouldn't have been able to attend, anyway. My parents were much too poor for that. The first books I read about filmmaking were books I had stolen. I remember walking into this bookstore and sliding the Hitchcock book by Truffaut inside a long trench coat. I'm not too proud of it, but, well, that's how I learned film theory. I also snuck my way into movie theaters. And I went to see a lot of films. I have to say, Hong Kong was a great place for a moviegoer to be in those days. Because of the geographic location, we were equally influenced by the European, Japanese, and American cinema. We approached the French New Wave on the same level as Hollywood B movies. To us, they were all equal. We didn't feel like we had to choose one over the other. I made no distinction between a Jacques Demy film or a Sam Peckinpah film. And that probably makes my films so different today—there's the influence of both.

Anyway, I quickly became crazy about films. With a group of young people, I decided to make a short 16-millimeter movie. To this day, it probably remains the most experimental film I've ever made. It was a love story: a man loves a woman so much that he ties her up, she dies, and eventually she turns into a butterfly and flies away. It was meant as a reflection on beauty, love, and freedom. And the result was pretty bad, to tell the truth. But it helped me get my first job in the industry.

EXTREME METHODS

I don't rely on any rules. When I shoot a scene, I try all sorts of angles. I cover everything, from wide shot to close-up, and then I choose in the editing, because that's the moment when I know how I really feel about the scene. At that point, I usually relate to my characters so much that I can *feel* the movie and make the right decisions from sheer instinct. So I never hesitate to shoot a scene with several cameras (sometimes up to fifteen at a time, for really complex action scenes) and also to use some of them at different speeds. My favorite slow-motion speed is 120 frames per second. That's one-fifth the normal speed. The reasons for these slow-motion shots is that if I feel a moment is either particularly dramatic or exceptionally real, I try to capture it and make it last as long as possible. But these are things I don't necessarily know on the set. I usually discover them during the editing. It's like a truth that is revealed to me, that I suddenly feel so strongly about that I will want to emphasize it. For example, even if I have covered a scene with many different angles, maybe I will find it is so emotional that I need to stay close to the actor. So I will use only the close-up and throw away all the rest. That can happen. It depends on the mood.

In any case, I tend to rely on only two kinds of lenses to compose my frames: very wide angle and extreme telephoto. I use the wide angle because when I want to see something, I want to see it completely, with the most detail possible. As for the telephoto, I use it for close-ups because I find it creates a real "encounter" with the actor. If you shoot someone's face with a 200-millimeter lens, the audience will feel like the actor is really standing in front of them. It gives presence to the shot. So I like extremes. Anything in between is of no interest to me.

There is something else that is, I guess, specific to my films: I tend to have trouble moving the camera in scenes that are not strictly action. The only two exceptions to that might be *The Killer* and *Face/Off*. And I think that is what makes me so proud of these films. Because in both cases, the camera movements work a little like music, like an opera—not too long, not too fast, always at the right moment. There are great camera moves in *Hardboiled*, but only in action sequences, whereas in *Face/Off* and *The Killer*, it didn't matter whether it was a dramatic scene or action. All the camera moves seemed in the same tone and at the same speed.

I LIKE TO CREATE ON THE SET

People always talk about the Hong Kong studios being particularly harsh, and to some extent this is true, because all they care about is the money. The Hong Kong audience is a very greedy one; they always want more. And so the studios have to feed that. However, if you give the studios a film that has commercial value, you can work the way you want. They leave you alone; you have creative freedom. When I worked there, I never even screened my dailies to the studio. I just delivered the final product, often late and over budget. But as long as the film made money, they didn't complain.

In Hollywood, it's a different story. What surprised me the most when I started working there was how many people were involved in the creative process. Too many people with too many ideas. Too many meetings, too much politics, too little risk taking. It takes an enormous amount of energy to still want to shoot after that. And the problem is that I rely heavily on instinct; I like to create on the set. I never did a shot list; I never storyboarded a scene. Well, I do it now to a certain extent, to reassure the studios, but I never use it, really, because . . . how can I explain? You see, if I love a woman, I cannot love her in my imagination; I need to see her in flesh and bone to get real feelings. It's the same with a scene. Theory means nothing to me. I have to be on the actual set to be inspired.

So usually, the first thing I like to see is how the actors move, how they deal with the scene. And I combine that with my own ideas. I do a rough rehearsal. Here's how I approach it: if the scene is about, let's say, loneliness, I ask the actor to play that in a very abstract manner. I will say something like, "Go over by the window and feel lonely. Forget the scene, forget the character, forget everything else, just think about how you act when you're lonely." I find that helps the actors bring out true feelings based on their own lives and project them onto their characters to create a true moment. Maybe the actor won't feel comfortable by the window and will decide to come sit in a corner or lie down. At some point, I will get the feeling that something is right, that it rings true, and I will go with that. And maybe that means that I will change the scene completely. But I do that first, and it is only once I have it that I set up the camera. It is very instinctive; it resembles the way a painter works, maybe. And I guess you can easily understand why it worries the studios.

WATCH THE ACTORS' EYES

I think if you want to work with actors, first of all, you have to fall in love with them. If you hate them, don't even bother. This is something I understood very early on, when I saw

Truffaut's *Day for Night.* I was amazed to see how much he cared about his actors. And so that's what I try to do, too; I treat actors as though they're part of my family. Before I start shooting, I insist on spending a lot of time with them. We talk a lot, and I try to see how they feel about life, what kinds of ideas they have, what kinds of dreams. We talk about what they love and what they hate. I try to discover what each actor's main quality is because this is what I'll try to emphasize in the film. And usually, as actors are talking to me, I start looking at them to try to find the best camera angle for them. Does this actor look better from this side or that side, from above or from below? I observe them in detail.

After that, once we actually start working, there are two primary things. First, of course, is communication with the actor. And to achieve that, I always try to find something that he or she and I have in common. Maybe it's something philosophical—we have the same moral values. Or maybe it's something more trivial—we both like soccer. But it's very important because often the whole communication process will rest on that. It's something you can always fall back on when conflicts arise. The other thing I pay a lot of attention to is the eyes. When an actor acts, I always stare at his or her eyes. Always. Because it tells me if he or she is being truthful or just faking it.

AN INVISIBLE MUSIC

Music is important in my films. And I'm not talking about the score of the film. When I'm preparing a scene, I like to listen to a certain kind of music. It can be classical, it can be rock and roll, whatever helps me get into the mood of the scene. In fact, very often, when I shoot a scene, I don't really listen to the dialogue; I keep listening to the music. I mean, if they're good actors, I know they'll deliver their lines. But I like the performance to match the music because it's the mood I'm interested in. After that, when I work in the editing room, I use that same music to cut the picture. It's the music that gives the rhythm and the pace of the scene.

That's part of the reason I use so many camera angles and so many speeds. If the music climaxes, I will need a shot in extreme slow motion to match it, and so on. Then, once the film is edited, that music disappears. Either I have a new score composed or I keep the scene without music, just dialogue. But in a way, the original music is still there. It's there like a ghost, like something invisible—or, actually, inaudible— which gives the scene a life of its own.

I MAKE FILMS FOR MYSELF

There are two main reasons why I make movies. First, because I always had trouble communicating with people, so films are a way for me to create a bridge between myself and the rest of the world. And second, because I like to explore, to discover things about people and myself.

One thing I'm particularly interested in is trying to find what two apparently very different people can turn out to have in common. Which is why it's a recurrent theme in my films. It's something I like to explore, and in that sense, I guess I make films for myself. Even when I'm on the set, I never think about the audience. I never ask myself whether they're going to like the film or not; I never try to anticipate how they will react. I don't think I should, either.

When you make a film, everything should come from the heart—which means you should always tell the truth. Well, at least, *your* truth. I think that's why so many people are touched by the films I make, because I try to make them with honesty. I also try to make them the best I can. Ever since I started directing, I have always struggled to make the perfect film. But I still don't feel that I have. So I have to move on to the next film . . . to once again attempt to create the ideal movie.

Films: *Young Dragon* (1973), *The Dragon Tamers* (1974), *Princess Cheung Ping* (1975), *Countdown in Kung Fu* (1975), *Money Crazy* (1977), *Follow the Star* (1977), *Last Hurrah for Chivalry* (1978), *From Rags to Riches* (1979), *To Hell with the Devil* (1981), *Laughing Times* (1981), *Plain Jane to the Rescue* (1982), *Heroes Shed No Tears* (1983, released in 1986), *The Time You Need a Friend* (1984), *Run, Tiger, Run* (1985), *A Better Tomorrow* (1986), *A Better Tomorrow Part 2* (1987), *The Killer* (1989), *Just Heroes* (1990), *Bullet in the Head* (1990), *Once a Thief* (1991), *Hardboiled* (1992), *Hard Target* (1993), *Broken Arrow* (1996), *Face/Off* (1997), *Mission: Impossible 2* (1999)

NEW BLOOD

Joel and Ethan Coen
Takeshi Kitano
Emir Kusturica
Lars Von Trier
Wong Kar-wai

Of the twenty-one filmmakers in this book, these six are probably the ones who have been considered most at the vanguard of filmmaking over the last ten years. The international make-up of the group may be more accidental than anything else. However, the fact that the only Americans in this category are independent filmmakers is not a surprise, as the most original work that has emerged over the last decade has been made by independents rather than big film studios.

JOEL AND ETHAN COEN
Joel Coen, b. 1954; Ethan Coen, b. 1957, Minneapolis, Minnesota

Joel and Ethan Coen have often conceded that they are the worst interviewees you can imagine. They're at a loss when it comes to explaining their films and will often answer questions with, at best, "I don't know" or, at worst, an embarrassed shrug.

For a journalist who sometimes has to restrain people from speaking too much, this can be a little awkward. The first time I met the Coen brothers, I left the room in a cold sweat because I knew there was nothing they had told me that I could use in print. When I interviewed them a second time, I spent a few hours sharpening my questions, and the result was significantly better. So when we met a third time for this master class, I knew precisely what I had to ask and how to do it. They are accustomed to hiding behind the standard "We do everything out of instinct" response, which I'm sure is partially true. But there is so much thinking involved in their films, be it conscious or not, that I couldn't let their explanation rest at that.

We met in Paris at the time The Big Lebowski *was being released. The huge success of* Fargo *two years earlier hadn't changed them a bit: they still behaved like two craftsmen who made personal films in their little shop, one after the next, with no other objective than personal satisfaction. And that may be what makes them so genuinely sympathetic. For practical reasons, I've separated the two brothers' answers. The actual conversation would have been impossible to transcribe because Joel and Ethan are so incredibly in synch that they systematically finish each other's sentences.*

▓ Master Class with Joel and Ethan Coen

Joel: Teaching is not something we've ever really considered. There is a selfish reason for that—it would take too much of our time and prevent us from working on our projects—but also a more pragmatic one, which is that we would probably have no idea what to tell the students. We're not the most articulate filmmakers around, mostly when it comes to explaining what we do and how we do it. Sometimes we go to film schools, show one of our films, and answer some of the questions the students might have. But they tend to be very specific questions, which rarely have to do with the craft itself. Most of the time, really, film students are looking for advice on how to raise money.

Ethan: I guess one way to teach could be to show films. Though, once again, our tastes are not what you might call classical. In fact, most of the films we love and that have inspired us are obscure movies that most people consider terrible. I remember when we worked with Nicolas Cage on *Raising Arizona*, we talked about his uncle, Francis Ford Coppola, and told him that *Finian's Rainbow*, which hardly anyone has ever seen, was one of our favorite films. He told his uncle, who I think has considered us deranged ever since. So anyway, if we did show these kinds of films in a classroom, it might get a good laugh but might not necessarily teach anyone how to make a good film. Though I guess getting exposed to different kinds of filmmaking, and becoming more open-minded about cinema, is one of the advantages of going to film school.

Joel: The other advantage of film school is that it does give you some experience in dealing with the chaos of the set. It's all on a much smaller scale, of course. You're dealing with crews of five to ten people, budgets of a few hundred dollars. But the general sense of how things work, and the dynamic you have to deal with in terms of people and time, and even money, isn't that much different.

Ethan: Joel went to film school, but I didn't. I learned the basics, the nuts and bolts of how a film gets made, by working as an assistant editor and then, eventually, as an editor. And I think that's actually a very good way to learn because going through all this raw material lets you see firsthand the way a director took a script and broke it down. You get to see what good coverage is and what bad coverage is. You see all the shots that are useless, and you understand why. Also, it gives you a good idea of what actors do. You see the raw material and you see them do take after take after take, and you can observe how they evolve. In my view, it really is the best learning experience you can have. Short of actually making a film, of course.

MAKING MOVIES IS A BALANCING ACT

Ethan: I'm tempted to say that the biggest lesson we learned about filmmaking is that there is no net, which is a line from David Mamet's *Speed-the-Plow*. But I guess the main lesson is that you have to remain flexible. You have to remain open-minded and accept that sometimes you can't get what you want. You can't be too married to your own ideas. Well . . . that's not quite true: there has to be a sort of *central* idea that you're after, that you're aware of and that you don't let circumstances distract you from. And there is a danger, actually, of letting yourself be seduced from the original idea that got you interested in the movie. And there is often a lot of pressure to alter your ideas because something is going to be too difficult to achieve, logistically or financially . . . And you have to know when to resist that.

Joel: That's true, making movies is a balancing act. On the one hand, you need to be open to new ideas if the reality of the situation requires it and not rigidly try to reproduce your original ideas. But on the other hand, you must have enough confidence in your own ideas so that you're not changing in response to any sort of exterior exigency that will want to make you push the movie one way or another. But there are no lessons, really, no rules that you can rely on. It's always a fluid situation where you have to kind of use your instincts.

Ethan: Since we're controlling the film pretty much from beginning to end, it's easy to keep on doing what we want to do. However, reality always remains an obstacle. You get to the set and a scene doesn't work the way you planned it, or the light doesn't look like what you wanted . . . And the fact that we do our own thing makes everything we want even more specific and precise. So circumstances are even more likely to not give us what we want.

THE SCRIPT IS JUST A STEP

Joel: It's hard to say where our original desire comes from, whether it's the writing or the images. Our interest is in stories, that's certain. We like telling stories. But we don't see the writing as the best form to do that. It's just a step. We really think in terms of images.

Ethan: The main difference for us between the writing and the directing is that we're willing to write for other people but we wouldn't direct a script that has been written by somebody else. Part of it comes from a purely pragmatic point of view: writing a script takes a few weeks, sometimes a few months. Directing a film can take up to two years of our lives. So it better be worth it!

Joel: Also, writing for other people is an interesting exercise. It gives you an opportunity to work on material that is interesting but that you wouldn't consider filming yourselves. It's a way to experiment in a relatively safe way. We don't even mind getting rewrite notes from studios, whereas we would never accept it on one of our own films. Because when you write for hire, it becomes a problem-solving game. And we have fun doing it.

Ethan: When we work on our own films, however, we really try to shut out outside points of view. And we don't test much, we don't show work in progress, because we find that you can get really conflicting information from that process. The major thing you're concerned about, really, is clarity. And that's a hard thing to determine by yourself. It's really like looking at two color cards and asking yourself, "Does this one work better than the other?" rather than showing it to a bunch of people and asking, "Which do you like better?" Of course, you're not really making the film for yourself; you're always making it for some audience, but it's a very generic audience for us. It's kind of an abstract audience. When we're on the set making decisions, we're always wondering whether a scene works or not, whether it's going to play or not, and really, we're wondering that in regard to the audience, not for us specifically. But it has to work for us too. In fact, it has to work for us *first*, I guess!

YOUR VISION SHIFTS A LITTLE EVERY DAY

Joel: When we start writing a script, we don't necessarily know what it's about, or what form it's going to take, or where it's going to go, and it comes to life little by little. It's true with the movie too, but in a slightly different way. With us, the finished movie probably resembles the script more than with most directors, mainly because we tend to shoot the script and not revise it extensively in production. But on the other hand, there are so many subtle changes, every day, that the movie really becomes different at the end from what you originally had in mind. Everything has kind of shifted, and you usually can't even remember what your original vision was.

Ethan: Filmmaking has its own grammar, just as literature does. Everybody knows what basic coverage should be, and just because you have some kind of idiosyncratic ideas that might work even though they're breaking the rules, the fact remains that there are rules that are there and that work. There is such a thing as a conventional way to cover a scene. A good director knows what the most basic way to cover is, and I guess most will try to go for that. But of course, following the rules does not guarantee that the film will work. That would be too easy.

Joel: We usually storyboard most of the shots. But when we get on the set in the morning, we start by rehearsing with the actors. We walk around the set with them a lot, and usually they sort of figure out the best blocking among themselves, depending on what is most comfortable or most interesting. After that, we go to the director of photography and decide, from what we've seen of the acting, how much we want to stick to the storyboard or not. And most of the time, we'll ignore it because the blocking of the scene makes the storyboard academic.

Ethan: We know pretty much exactly how we want to shoot each scene. Sometimes exactly, and usually at least roughly. How much we actually cover depends on a lot of things. We frequently shoot scenes—especially in our most recent movies, and particularly in *Fargo*—that have no coverage at all because they're done in one shot. And in other scenes we do so much coverage that we look at each other at the end of the day like we're a couple of morons who've never made movies!

Joel: I guess we tend to cover more at the beginning of the film, because it's usually been a long time and we're a little nervous and afraid. And then, as we get back into the rhythm, we become more confident.

A WIDER APPROACH

Ethan: We're not particularly purist about anything technical. We're ready to try anything. Although, in terms of lenses, we probably tend to use wider lenses than most directors. That's always been true. One of the reasons for that is that we love moving the camera, and wide lenses make the moves much more dynamic. And they give a longer depth of field. On the other hand, the longer lenses tend to be more flattering to actors, and though I know it is a concern to most directors, I have to confess it's never really been the case for us. Our new director of photography, Roger Deakins, whom we've been working with since *Barton Fink*, is slowly trying to change that. I don't think he had ever used a wider lens than a 25-millimeter before working with us. And I don't think we'd ever used anything longer than a 40-millimeter, which most people already consider pretty wide.

Joel: The two films we probably experimented the most on were *Blood Simple* and *Barton Fink*. *Blood Simple*, because it was the first one and so everything had the virtue of novelty. And to tell the truth, we weren't quite sure what we were doing. *Barton Fink,* because it is the most stylized film we've made and also because it faced us with the question, How do you make a film about a guy in a room, pretty much, and still make it interesting and compelling? It was a real challenge. But *The Hudsucker Proxy* was also an experiment in extreme artificiality, and *Fargo* was an experiment in a sort of extreme reality—which was a fake reality, because it was as stylized as the other ones. Compared to all that, the films we're making today are not real adventures. Not that we don't like the way they look, but they're all stuff we've done before, pretty much.

THE BEST ACTORS BRING THEIR OWN IDEAS

Joel: Neither of us has any acting background; we sort of came to filmmaking from the technical end or the writing end, as opposed to someone who comes from the theater and has experience working with actors. So we hadn't worked with professional actors when we made our first film, and I remember that we had very specific notions of what a line should sound like, or how a reading should be done. But as you get a little more experienced and start having a little more fun with it, you realize that you have one idea and it may not be the best idea. And that's what you hire the actors to do, to improve on your conception—not just to mimic it but to expand it, to create something of their own which you couldn't have imagined yourself.

Ethan: Working with actors is really a two-way system. And the director doesn't tell them what to do as much as explain to them what he wants so that the actors can adapt to that, to help them out. Because you're not there to teach them how to act. You're there to give them what makes them comfortable, to give them the kinds of things they're looking for from you. Sometimes they'll want to talk a lot *around* what you're doing but not specifically about it. Or sometimes it's just "Tell me where to stand and how fast to talk." So it's a question of getting a feeling in the first few days of what their process is, to be sensitive about that. And maybe that means to stay out of their way.

Joel: Actors like to work in all different kind of ways. No question about that. But the really easy actors to work with from a visual point of view are the ones who have their own ideas, which may not conform to how you imagine a scene being blocked or may not fit into what your visual plan was for the scene. But they tell you what their ideas are. And they're also sensitive to a certain extent to what you're trying to do visually. Jeff Bridges, for instance, is very much like that. He'll adapt his ideas to your vision. He has his own thing, but he can work it around to compromise with your ideas.

Ethan: Of course, casting is important. And you have to be open to surprises. Sometimes you cast someone obvious, and sometimes you have to take a risk to get something more interesting. For instance, *Miller's Crossing* wasn't written for an Irishman. But Gabriel Byrne came in and said he thought it would sound pretty good with an Irish accent. And I know I was thinking, "Yeah, right." But then he did it, and we realized it did sound pretty good. And so we changed the part. Same with William H. Macy for *Fargo*. We had in mind the total opposite: someone kind of fat and a little schleppy. But Bill came in and made us totally reimagine the character. That's why we often like to see actors read, even if we know their work, because that kind of thing does happen.

Joel: Once we've cast and have started working on the set, though, we're not too open to surprises anymore. We don't like to let actors improvise, for instance. That isn't to say that actors don't sometimes rewrite lines or come up with their own lines, but that's different from improvisation. The only time we do actual improvisation is during rehearsals, to bring certain things out, but that usually doesn't affect the scene itself. What we'll usually do is ask the actors to invent the parts of the scene that aren't written, the five minutes that take place before and after the scene. We find that it helps them get into the scene better. Jeff Bridges and John Goodman liked to do that a lot on *The Big Lebowski*. And sometimes it was very funny. Actually, sometimes it was even better than what we wrote!

Films: *Blood Simple* (1984), *Raising Arizona* (1987), *Miller's Crossing* (1990), *Barton Fink* (1991), *The Hudsucker Proxy* (1994), *Fargo* (1996), *The Big Lebowski* (1998), *O Brother, Where Art Thou?* (2000), *The Man Who Wasn't There* (2001)

TAKESHI KITANO
b. 1948, Tokyo, Japan

Doing an interview with a translator is always a little complicated, but in the case of Takeshi Kitano, it bordered on the surreal. The director, who has often played gangsters in his own films, has a stony face and a deep voice that, added to the harshness of his Japanese accent, makes his answers sound dogmatic and terse. Once translated, however, they turn out to be either ironic or self-deprecating. Kitano is actually incapable of saying something without making it into some sort of joke. But he does it with such a poker face that you don't dare laugh; you feel as though he might kill you if you don't nod respectfully.

We met at the Cannes Film Festival, where he had come to show Kikujiro's Summer, *a comedy that disappointed most critics, mainly, I think, because it was a comedy. Although Kitano made his debut as a comic on Japanese TV, it was mainly through a series of dark, violent, and lyrical films that his work became noticed around the world as a Japanese alternative to what was already being done in the same genre in Hong Kong. He quickly gained a group of hard-core fans, but his commercial success remained marginal until, against all odds, he received the Grand Prize at the quite cerebral Venice Film Festival in 1998 for* Hana-Bi. *The film, whose title means "Fireworks" in Japanese, is indeed one of great visual beauty, and it made everyone realize what a true artist Takeshi Kitano is.*

▨ Master Class with Takeshi Kitano

Rather than give classes, I've been tempted for a while now by the idea of writing a book in which I'd use my experiences as a director to share ideas, outline theories, and give advice, both about the visuals and directing actors, to people who haven't yet made a film. The only thing stopping me, I have to admit, is fear of ridicule. If a great artist like Akira Kurosawa gives lessons after his impressive career, that's perfectly normal. But I have directed only a handful of films so far, and if I start playing the professor, I know what people will say: "Come on, who do you think you are?" So I'm waiting awhile. But I will do it one day.

A SUCCESSION OF PERFECT IMAGES

It is not a coincidence that I referred to Kurosawa. If students were to ask me, "What's a great film?" I'd immediately send them to see *Kagemusha, The Seven Samurai,* or *Rashomon.* The amazing thing about Kurosawa's films, I find, is the precision of the image. In the framing and the placing of the characters, the composition is always perfect, even when the camera is moving. You could easily take each one of the twenty-four frames in every second and it would make a beautiful picture. I think that's the ideal definition of cinema: a succession of perfect images. And Kurosawa is the only director who has attained that.

At my level, I'm happy if I can find only two or three images, maybe not perfect but in any case very powerful, to form the foundations of the film. For example, in *Kikujiro's Summer,* I knew even before writing the screenplay that I wanted to include the moment when the character I play walks off alone along the beach and the child runs after him to take his hand. This image, as well as a few others, was my reason for making that particular film. With that in mind, I invented a plot and wrote scenes to create a link between the images. But in the end, the story is almost an excuse. My cinema is much more a cinema of images than a cinema of ideas.

BEGINNINGS, GOOD AND BAD SURPRISES

To finish with Kurosawa, I'll just say that my dream would have been to borrow the dailies of his films to see the way in which, take after take, he had corrected things to reach such a perfect final result. Unfortunately, I wasn't able to do that.

In fact, my training as a director took place in a fairly odd and unplanned way. I was working a lot for TV as a show host in front of the camera—or *cameras*, actually, since there were usually at least six in the studio. I started to understand the relationship that the camera created with space and the actors. Little by little, I started having my own ideas of what directing should be, and after a while, I no longer agreed with the decisions of the people directing me. I'd say, "No, that camera should be filming instead of this one, and from that angle rather than this!" Then I started directing the shows myself, while remaining in front of the camera. My directing work for TV wasn't very good despite all this—far from it—but very soon I felt like moving on to the big screen. However, I came up against a huge and unexpected problem: credibility.

On my first film, the crew simply didn't trust me. I guess they probably saw me as a TV star fulfilling a whim by making a movie. In any case, I remember arriving on the set the first day and asking the cameraman to set up the first shot. He looked at me warily and asked, "Why do you want to shoot it like that? Why don't you start with an establishing shot?" I told him that it was a matter of intuition, that I didn't feel I needed an establishing shot in that scene. But that didn't suit him. He insisted that I should give my reasons. I could tell that the whole crew was just as wary as he was. He had another idea in mind, and I had to fight him for an hour before winning the point. It wasn't a very important shot—in fact, it ended up on the cutting-room floor—but it was a matter of principle. I had to impose my credibility as a filmmaker. And that lasted throughout the shoot.

The other thing that surprised me the most about my first film was the unbelievable number of constraints—financial, temporal, human, and artistic—that could rise up between the director's vision and the final result. I thought that a director's job was, above all, to have good ideas. I realized instead that it mainly consisted of managing all kinds of outside elements to create the right environment to bring those ideas to fruition.

A FILM IS A TOY BOX

Cinema is something very personal. When I make a film, I make it first and foremost for myself. It's like a wonderful toy box that I play with. A very expensive toy box, of course, and I'm ashamed at times of having such fun with it. There comes a time, however, once the film is in the can, when it no longer belongs to you. It then becomes the toy of the audience—and the critics. But it would be dishonest to deny that I make a film for myself before anyone else.

Actually, that's why I can't understand how a director can shoot a film from someone else's screenplay, since the cinema is something much too personal for that, unless you have a great deal of freedom to adapt the screenplay—in which case I truly think that the director must take it over completely and make it virtually his own screenplay. This intimately personal side to the cinematic vision constitutes both the strength and the weakness of a director. I have already heard many directors say this, and the same holds true for me: with each new film, I try to do something totally different. But when I look at the end result, I realize that I have made exactly the same film all over again. Perhaps not exactly the same one, but I think that if a police inspector were to see it, he would say, "No doubt about it, Kitano, you're behind this; your prints are all over it!"

MAKING DECISIONS, EVEN ARBITRARY ONES

My main priority in any given scene is the composition of the image. Possibly even more than the actors' performances. This is why I always begin by setting up the camera. When I arrive on the set in the morning, I don't always have a concrete idea of what I want to shoot, but I know that I need to make a quick decision because the crew is there behind me, waiting impatiently for me to tell them what to do. If I start walking around to look for inspiration, they won't let me go; they'll follow me. Once, on a film that we were shooting in the mountains, I slipped away for a few minutes because I needed to be alone to think, and when I settled down in what seemed to be a quiet spot, I realized that the whole crew had obediently followed me. They were very upset when I told them to go away and leave me alone. So when I arrive in the morning, if after about ten minutes I haven't had a brainwave, I make an arbitrary decision. I say, "We'll set up here." So the crew sets up and positions the camera; then we bring on the actors. We do a run-through, and, of course, nine times out of ten, it doesn't work. But in the meantime, I've had time to think and can suggest a better configuration. I might make the crew move three or four times like this before getting what I like, but it's better than leaving them hanging around waiting.

On the other hand, once I find the angle that I like, I cover myself very little or even not at all. I choose one way of film-ing a scene and I stick to it, even if I end up regretting it during editing, which happens at times. As long as the cam-eraman doesn't start kicking up a fuss, I don't try anything else. From time to time, this makes him a little nervous. In the past, he'd ask me, for safety's sake, to try shooting with two or three cameras. I did it to reassure him, but I realized during editing that I was almost always using shots from the main camera, the one that I had chosen. So I stopped doing that.

However, I think a director needs to be very vigilant, not in relation to what he asks the cameraman to shoot—after all, it's his job—but in relation to all the accidental, spontaneous, or chance things that can occur around the set and that a direc-tor can seize on to use in the film. On *Fireworks*, we were set-ting up a scene on the beach when I saw some large fish leaping above the waves out at sea. I immediately told the cameraman to film them. I couldn't explain why on a con-crete level, but I had the feeling that it was necessary, that this shot would fit into the film perfectly. When a surprise like this works, it provides the biggest satisfaction.

TRY EVERYTHING—ALMOST

Cinema has its fundamental rules that have been drawn up throughout its history by a large number of brilliant filmmak-ers. However, I believe that rather than respect them, each filmmaker must adapt these rules to a personal way of filming, which generally means altering them or breaking them.

I know, for instance, that in film schools—in Japanese ones, anyway—students are always taught that what the cam-era films must represent someone's point of view. But at times, I film characters from a high angle, looking down on them, even though there's no one above them. And it works. No one ever asks me if it's the vision of God or a bird. The audience finds it normal. On one film, I shot a take from a low angle after a shoot-out and the cameraman didn't understand. He told me, "That's impossible! That means the corpse is seeing this, but he's dead." It shocked him a great deal. But that was the way I sensed it, and it never surprised anyone in the audience.

On the other hand, there are things that I quite simply refuse to do. One thing I hate in films is when the camera starts circling the characters. If three people are sitting at a table talking, you'll often see the camera circling them. I can't explain why, but I find it totally fake. I'm often accused of not taking advantage of all the possibilities of the camera, but I refuse to use that particular movement. And yet—this will probably make you smile—one thing I want to try one day is to place the camera in the middle of the table and to rotate it between the characters, as if it were on a lazy Susan in a Chinese restaurant. Therefore, I'm ready to rotate the camera *in front of* the characters but not *behind* them. Why? I cannot say.

The most experimental of my films in its approach was *Sonatine*. When I shot it, I was really worried that people would think I was totally crazy, but that mainly concerned the content. Where form is concerned, the film on which I have tried out the most ideas is probably *Kikujiro*. For instance, I amused myself by filming the dragonfly's point of view. And then there's the shot in the bar where the waitress's head is framed just above the head on the beer. This isn't necessarily a successful shot, but I wanted to try it. There's also the scene when the two angels leave. I wanted to shoot the reflection of the little boy in the hubcap of the departing wheel. I tried it, but it gave the opposite impression: it looked as if the kid was leaving while the hubcap was staying. Too bad.

CHOOSE ACTORS TO PLAY AGAINST TYPE

I never work with famous actors because I find that almost dangerous for the kind of films I make. A famous actor generally brings such a powerful image with him that it's likely to unbalance the film and therefore hamper it rather than help it. Moreover, when I pick my actors, I avoid choosing people specialized in a particular kind of part because they are likely to have developed tics in their performance that are impossible to correct. So, for instance, to play gangsters, I never choose actors who have already played gangsters in other films. On the contrary, I pick people who are used to playing office staff—and the result is all the more surprising. The reason I also appear in my own films is that I have a very personal approach to time, which means that, for instance, I never speak exactly when people expect me to. I'm always a little out of synch. And while I can do this myself, I'm incapable of telling someone else how to pull off these moments of inner performance that are very important in my films.

Directing actors is something that is both simple and complex. I believe that the secret is to avoid giving the lines to the actors too soon. In fact, it's best that they don't even have them the previous day. Otherwise, they're going to rehearse them alone, shooting their own film in their minds, imagining things. Once they're on the set, when I give them my instructions, they'll be unsettled because things won't match what they've prepared. So, most of the time, I give them their lines just before shooting, hoping that they'll have time to memorize them. And often, my best instruction in terms of performance is "Act as you would in daily life . . . except you're dressed differently."

ASIA VERSUS AMERICA

I don't really know where I stand as a filmmaker. When I look at Asian cinema in general, and Japanese cinema in particular, I often feel as if I'm looking at a peasant who has come up to the city wearing his best clothes but who doesn't feel comfortable in them.

All the same, this doesn't mean that I feel closer to American cinema. It's too standardized, too dogmatic—there has to be a hero, a family, black people, meal scenes, and so on. It's extremely restrictive. And besides, Asian cinema can do something that American cinema is unable to do: control the use of time. In a Hollywood movie, if there are more than ten seconds of silence, people freak out. In Asia, we have a more natural and healthier relationship with time. In the end, it's also a question of scale. For Americans, having a good time means building a Disneyland, whereas I have the impression that we can still have a good time with a simple Ping-Pong game. In the end, I guess money is what governs each culture's style of shooting, and that's a pity.

Films: *Violent Cop* (1989), *Boiling Point* (1990), *A Scene by the Sea* (1992), *Sonatine* (1993), *Getting Any?* (1994), *Kids Return* (1996), *Fireworks* (1997), *Kikujiro's Summer* (1999), *Brother* (2000)

EMIR KUSTURICA
b. 1954, Sarajevo, Yugoslavia

In a career of only six films, Emir Kusturica has managed to receive, not only once, but twice, the Grand Prize at the Cannes Film Festival, one of the most coveted awards for any film director. But perhaps the most impressive thing about Kusturica is how detached he is from success. Most of the interviews in this book took place in hotel rooms or quiet, secluded suites. But when we met as he was releasing Black Cat, White Cat, *he suggested we do it in the café below his apartment in Paris. I was afraid we might be disturbed every five minutes by people who would recognize him, but that didn't happen.*

Kusturica the man may not be immediately recognizable, but his films most certainly are. If you've never seen one, try to imagine something between a three-ring Gypsy circus and a surreal magic act. You probably can't, and that's what makes this Yugoslavian-born director so original. It might be tempting to think that all his organized chaos is more chaotic than organized, that chance had a big part in the making of such poetic and unpredictable films. But as you will see from his lesson, while Emir Kusturica is driven by the mysterious wildness of his Slavic soul, he definitely has all the rigor and precision that Eastern European directors are famous for.

▨ Master Class with Emir Kusturica

The idea of teaching someone how to make a film is both very ambitious and very exciting but, in my opinion, not very realistic. I taught film for two years at Columbia University in New York and came away with the feeling that it's impossible to give anyone any real pointers about the way to make a film. However, I think that it is possible to screen certain films and analyze them, with precise examples of scenes or shots, to show how each filmmaker uses his given talent to make a film.

Personally, I believe that the first and most important lesson for a future filmmaker is to learn to become an author, to learn to impose his or her own vision on the film. After all, cinema is a collaborative art where you continually deal with the doubts and divergent opinions of others. Young filmmakers often have a great many ideas but very little experience, and their ideas are soon shattered when they come up against the demands of reality. To avoid this, you have to be able to understand who you are, where you're from, and how all this experience can be translated into a filmic language.

For instance, if you take a look at Visconti's films, you will soon see how his directing style was influenced by the fact that he had staged operas. It's the same thing with Fellini: you can spot the draftsman behind the director. And it's obvious that the way I grew up on the streets of Sarajevo, continually in contact with people and fueled by avid energy and overflowing curiosity, has influenced my own way of filming. By studying each filmmaker's films, even the first five minutes, you see that they all have their own way of building up their work. If you then learn to distinguish and compare all these filmmakers' approaches, in the end you should be able to define your own.

MY PROGRAM

Each period in film history provides a different lesson for the person studying it. For instance, I always started off by showing my students Jean Vigo's *L'Atalante* because I feel that it represents the best possible balance between sound and image. It was shot in the early 1930s, a time when everything was still relatively new and image and sound were used with a great deal of caution and moderation. Now, when I see modern films, I'm struck by how both elements are abused. There's a systematic exaggeration that I find genuinely unhealthy.

After *L'Atalante*, I would generally move on to Jean Renoir's *La règle du jeu*, a film that I personally consider to be the cinema's greatest masterpiece in terms of direction. For me, this film is the peak of elegance in narration, with framing done in focal lengths that are neither too long nor too short, always adapted to human vision, with a great visual richness and a great depth of field. Moreover, it was Renoir—and even perhaps also his father, the painter—who influenced my manner of always creating very deep and very rich frames. Even when I shoot a close-up, something is always going on behind it; the face is always related to the world around it.

To get back to my program, I would then move on to the Hollywood melodramas of the 1930s and the amazing lessons that they can provide in terms of structure, simplicity, and narrative efficiency. There was also Russian cinema and its almost mathematical sense of direction, then postwar Italian cinema with Fellini and its way of linking perfect aesthetics with a sort of Mediterranean spirit that makes a film as vibrant and as attractive as a circus show. Finally, there was the American cinema of the 1960s and 1970s, an avant-garde and resolutely modern style of cinema that people like Spielberg and Lucas moved onto another plane in the 1980s.

BRINGING LIFE INTO THE IMAGE

The first films that I shot as a student were very linear. They had great rigor on an artistic level but weren't very exciting to watch. And I think that one of the main lessons I learned during my film studies in Czechoslovakia was the extent to which the cinema stands aside from all the other arts in terms of its collaborative aspect. I'm not only talking about the crew that makes the film but also about what is placed before the camera, what makes up the soul of the scene and brings it to life. I discovered as a director that I had a whole range of elements at my disposal that I could assemble as a sort of mosaic until a single spark brought the scene to life. There's something very musical about it, as if, in using very different kinds of sound, I were trying to create a melodious sensation in the audience's subconscious rather than transmitting a rational message.

This is why I spend a great deal of time preparing each shot and always run over on my shoots. I try to harmonize a whole range of different elements on a whole range of different levels until the required emotion finally comes across through the image. This is also why there is so much movement in my films. I hate the idea of revealing the characters' emotions through dialogue. I feel that expressing emotions through words rather than actions is an easy option that the cinema chooses more and more often. It's like a disease. Therefore, I try to let my actors speak as little as possible, and when they have to speak, I make sure that either they or the camera will be moving.

There's one scene in *Black Cat, White Cat* that I'm particularly fond of. It's the scene where the two actors cling to a rubber ring and confess their love for each other. The way I filmed the scene was to rotate the ring and accompany its movement with the camera. For me, it's this circular movement—the circle being the most perfect geometric shape in the world—that makes the shot magical rather than the words that the two characters are saying.

SUBJECTIVITY AS A PRINCIPLE

The worst mistake a young filmmaker can make is to believe that the cinema is an objective art. The only true way of being a filmmaker is not only to have a personal point of view but also to impose it on the film, at every level. You make your film and you make it for yourself, always with the hope, of course, that what you like about it will also be liked by others. If you try to make a film for the audience, you can't surprise them. And if you don't surprise them, then you can't make them think or evolve. Therefore, the film is first and foremost *your* film. Do you have to write the screenplay yourself to be the film's true auteur? I don't think so. On the contrary, I believe that you have a greater freedom of movement if all you do is film. I generally adapt someone else's screenplay, but on the set, I add so much of myself that I systematically take it over. The screenplay is merely a basis, a foundation that I lean on to build up the film's architecture. I never allow myself to be confined by the text; I remain open to the new ideas that the actors or the circumstances of the shoot provide, and above all, I always make sure that the film includes all kinds of very personal elements. That's why there are often hanged men, weddings, brass bands, and so forth in my films. These are my obsessions that regularly reappear, a little like swimming pools in Hockney's paintings. The elements are always the same, but I set them out differently each time in order to tell another story.

On a technical level, too, my directing is completely subjective. Each director necessarily faces a dilemma when it comes to setting up the camera. There's an artistic decision to be made based either on a logical and even moral explanation or on pure instinct. I always allow my instinct to guide me, but I understand that others find logic more reassuring. In any case, there isn't really a cinematic grammar. Or rather, there are hundreds of them, since each director invents his or her own.

THE CAMERA MUST DECIDE EVERYTHING

When I prepare a scene, I always start by positioning the camera, since I believe that directing involves first and foremost the control of space and what you want to see within that space. This is the basis of all cinema. Now, this control of space must be done through the camera. The actors must conform to the predetermined framing, not the other way around. First of all, for practical reasons, it's easier to ask an actor to adapt to visual constraints than to adapt the technical side to the actor's ideas. And then, because the camera helps the director direct the actors—in the sense that, if he knows how to impose it as the eye of the scene, he gives the actors a reference point that makes everything simple and clear. The camera is the director's ally since it is the source of his power; it's the point that he can base all his decisions on, however arbitrary.

In my opinion, the mistake that many novice directors make is to approach the cinema as a form of filmed theater; they are so respectful of the actors' work that they make it a priority and are unable to impose their visual point of view.

This attitude usually works against them, since actors need to be directed and need to be framed within set parameters. A director who allows actors free rein soon comes across as weak or indecisive, and that panics them.

At the same time, you must avoid being narrow-minded. And while it's very important to have a concrete approach to shooting a scene, it's also important to be receptive to surprises and ideas from the outside. While I always know what the scene I want to film looks like, I'm rarely able to guess what it will really be like in the end.

APPROACH EACH FILM AS IF IT WERE THE FIRST

A director really has only one aesthetic goal when making a film: to be stimulated by what he shoots. I know that a scene is good when I feel my heart beat faster, and the very reason I make films is to feel this kind of sensation. I need to be transported by the act of bringing the film into the world. And when I manage that, I believe that this feeling passes through the screen and that the audience will feel it in turn.

To achieve this, however, I think that you need to approach each film as if it were your very first. Avoid giving in to routine, and never stop exploring and evolving. With experience, it becomes very easy to fall back on old habits and to simply change lenses to create a new dynamic. But you really must stop yourself from doing that. For instance, I always refuse to cover a scene. I decide on a single way of shooting it and I stick to it, even if it means a real headache during editing. It's a continual challenge, but it forces me to think about the decisions I make on the set. And I don't hesitate to push each idea through to its conclusion. There are times when I could be content with the third take of a shot but I force myself to explore further, to enter the heart, the very substance of the scene. And that's how I end up shooting fifteen or twenty takes for one shot. It's a lot, I know. It's enormous. It's frightening for the producer. But when I found out that Stanley Kubrick was doing forty takes on his last film, that reassured me.

Films: *Do You Remember Dolly Bell?* (*Sjeccas li se, Dolly Bell*) (1981), *When Father Was Away on Business* (*Otac na sluzbenom putu*) (1985), *Time of Gypsies* (*Dom za vesanje*) (1989), *Arizona Dream* (1993), *Underground* (1995), *Black Cat, White Cat* (*Cma macka, beli macor*) (1998), *Super 8 Stories* (2001)

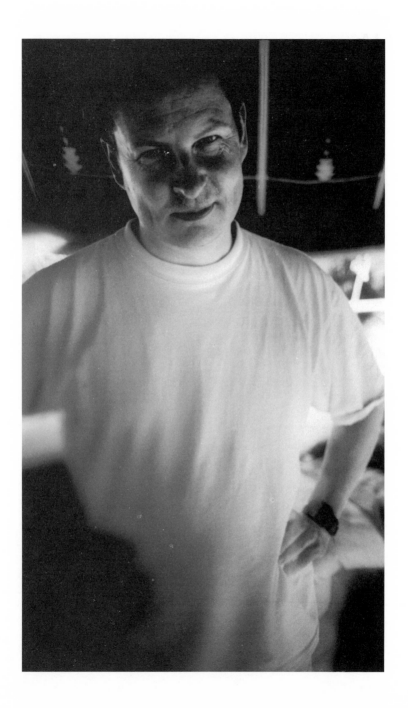

LARS VON TRIER
b. 1956, Copenhagen, Denmark

The word "compromise" does not mean much to Lars Von Trier. He's a man of extremes, and an eccentric to boot. Even though Breaking the Waves was officially entered at the 1996 Cannes Film Festival, he didn't attend because he was afraid to fly. His lead actress, Emily Watson, had to phone Von Trier live from the screening to let him hear the audience's reaction. When the director's next two films, The Idiots and Dancer in the Dark, were once again selected for Cannes, Von Trier made up his mind to make the long trip all the way across Europe from Denmark to the south of France . . . in a motor home.

As far as his films go, Von Trier also likes to go from one extreme to the other. If you look at his evolution as a director from The Element of Crime through Dancer in the Dark, there really is no logic other than a clear desire to continually reinvent cinema. In 1995, Lars Von Trier convinced a group of fellow Danish filmmakers to sign the Dogme 95 charter, a particularly strict set of rules and constraints that he and some colleagues pledged to apply on their films (see page 190). A few directors in other countries have followed suit, mostly after the success of Thomas Vinterberg's Celebration (Festen) in 1998. Most have stared at the charter in utter bewilderment.

I confess I expected to meet a rather didactic, aloof individual. Though I wouldn't call Lars Von Trier either easygoing or particularly warm, I was surprised that someone who clearly spends so much time thinking about the technical elements of cinema would have so much to say about film as a purely emotional experience.

◾ Master Class with Lars Von Trier

The reason I started making films, originally, was that I would see pictures in my head. I had these visions, which I felt compelled to translate through a camera. And I guess that's as good a reason as any to start making films. Today, however, it's totally different: I don't really have pictures in my head anymore, and making films has actually become a way for me to create these images. It's not my reason for making films that has changed but my approach to making them. I still see images, but they're abstract images, as opposed to before, when they were very concrete. I don't know how it happened; I think it's just a consequence of getting older, of maturing. I guess when you are younger, filmmaking is all about ideas and ideals, but then, as you get older, you start thinking more about life and have a different approach to your work, and that's what causes the change.

In spite of that, I have to say that to me, filmmaking has always been about emotions. What I notice about the great directors I admire is that if you show me five minutes of one of their films, I will know it is theirs. And even though most of my films are very different, I think I can claim the same thing, and I think it is the emotion that ties it all together.

In any case, I never set out to make a film to express a particular idea. I understand how one could see it that way with my first films, because they can appear a little cold and mathematical, but even then, deep down, it was always about emotions for me. The reason that the films I make today might appear stronger, emotionally speaking, is just that, as a person, I think I've become a better conveyor of emotions.

THE AUDIENCE? WHAT AUDIENCE?

I write my own scripts. I have no particular point of view on the author theory, although the only film that I adapted from a script written by somebody else is a film I don't like anymore. So I guess there is a difference between writing your own material and adapting someone else's. But as a director, you should be able to take a writer's work and make it completely yours. And on the other end, one could also claim that even when you write something yourself, it's always based on something that you've heard or seen, and so, in a way, it's not really yours. That's all a little arbitrary to me.

What I do feel strongly about, however, is that you have to make a film for yourself and not for the audience. If you start thinking about an audience, I think you will get lost and you will inevitably fail. Of course, you must have some desire to communicate to others, but to base the whole film on this will never work. You have to do a film because you want it, not because you think an audience wants it. That's a trap, and that's a trap I see a lot of directors falling into. I see a film and I know the director did it for the wrong reasons, that he didn't do it because he deeply wanted it.

That doesn't mean you can't make commercial films. It only means that you have to like the film before the audience does. A director like Steven Spielberg makes very commercial films, but I am sure that all the films he makes are films that he first and foremost wants to see himself. And that's why they work.

EACH FILM CREATES ITS OWN LANGUAGE

There is no grammar of filmmaking. Each film creates its own language. On the first films I directed, everything was storyboarded to the very last detail. In *Zentropa* (*Europa*), for instance, I think there wasn't a shot that wasn't storyboarded, because that was the peak of my "control freak" period. I was making very technical films, and I wanted to control every-thing, which made the shooting process really painful. And the results were not necessarily better. In fact, *Zentropa* is probably the film I dislike the most today.

The problem with wanting to control everything is that when you've storyboarded and planned everything, shooting it becomes nothing more than a duty. And the terrible part of it is that you can only end up achieving seventy percent—if you're lucky—of what you were dreaming of. Which is why the way I make films today is much better. On a film like *The Idiots*, for instance, I never spent time thinking how I was go-ing to shoot it until I was actually doing it. I never planned anything. I was just there, and I filmed what I was seeing. When you do that, you really start at zero, and everything that happens is a gift. So there's no frustration at all. Of course, that came from the fact that I was filming myself, and with a small video camera. So it was not really a camera anymore; it was my eye, it was me watching. If an actor said something to my right, I would just turn to him, and then turn back to the other actor when he answered, and then maybe turn to the left if I heard something happening there. Of course, there are things that you miss with this technique, but you have to make a choice. One of the great advantages of shooting with video is that time is no longer a factor. Some of the scenes that end up as one minute long in the film were one hour long when I shot them, which is a terrific way to work.* So for the time being, I will stick to video. It's fantastic to be able to just shoot and shoot and shoot. It makes rehearsals useless. I use the time before the shooting to discuss the characters,

---

*By "time," Von Trier really means film stock. It would be unthinkable—as well as technically impossible—to let a 35-millimeter camera roll for an hour to get a one-minute scene in the end. The cost alone would be astronomical.

and then the actors know from the script what the action is, and we start filming. And maybe we'll shoot it twenty times. And you don't really have to bother about it making any sense, visually speaking, until you're in the editing room.

EVERYONE HAS RULES

A lot of people seem to think that the rules of *Dogme 95* (see box on page 190) were created as a reaction to the way other people were making films, as if I were trying to put distance between them and me, to show that I was different. That's not the case. In fact, it couldn't be the case because, frankly, I have no idea how other people make films. I never go to see movies; I am totally ignorant of what is being done elsewhere. So these rules came more as a reaction to my own work, really. It was a way to trigger myself into doing more challenging things. It might sound very pretentious, but it's like if you're a juggler in a circus, and you start with three oranges, and after you've done that for a couple of years, you begin to think, "Hmmm, it would be nice if I were on a tightrope at the same time . . ." So it was a little bit of that kind of situation. I figured that by setting these rules, new experiences would come out, and that's precisely what happened.

To tell the truth, I have always been very strict about what I felt I could or could not do. And the rules of the Dogme are actually nothing compared to the unwritten rules I created for myself on a film like, let's say, *Element of Crime*. There is not a pan or a tilt in *Element of Crime*. I had forbidden myself to do that. I used only crane and dolly shots, and only separated, never mixed. There were many unspoken rules like that, which came out of, I don't know, a sick mind, I'm afraid! More seriously, I know it sounds very mechanical, but I think setting rules is a necessary approach to any film because the artistic process is a process of limitation. And

Dogme 95 is a series of strict rules designed in the spring of 1995 by a group of Danish directors (among them Lars Von Trier and Thomas Vinterberg, director of *Festen*). They "swore" to follow these rules on their subsequent films:

1. The film must take place only on actual location, and no set can be dressed [i.e., include artificial scenery]. You have to use what's on the location when you find it.

2. You must use only direct sound. And you can use music only if the CD player, tape player, radio, or live performers will be shown in the scene.

3. The camera must always be hand-held, even for still shots.

4. The film must be in color, and dramatic use of lighting is forbidden. There must be only enough light to see things properly.

5. No special effects of any kind are allowed.

6. No artificial action (murder, a gun, et cetera) can be introduced.

7. No manipulation of time and place is permitted.

8. Genre movies are not allowed.

9. The director must not be credited.

limitation means setting rules for yourself and for your film.

The difference with Dogme 95 is that we decided to put these rules on paper, and that may be why so many people were shocked. But I think most filmmakers, whether they are aware of it or not, have their own unwritten rules. And somehow I think that to put it on paper creates a certain honesty.

Because personally—and I guess it goes against most direc-tors' points of view—I like to see how a film is made. As a spectator, I like to somehow get a feeling as I'm watching it of the creative process that the film went through. And the rea-son I used tracking shots and cranes in *Element of Crime*, rather than pans and tilts, was that I didn't want to hide any-thing. A tracking shot is a big, obvious move, although in most American films, directors try to hide it. To them, it's just a convenient way to move from one point to another, so it has to be invisible. But I try to not hide how things are done. I feel like I would be cheating if I did. And in that regard, there was a big step when I stopped using the fixed camera and went to the hand-held camera. At the time, it was really an artistic de-cision. My editor had seen the TV series *Homicide*, which used hand-held cameras, and we both agreed that it would be good for my next movie, which was *Breaking the Waves*. So at first it was a stylistic consideration. But now I've gone beyond that, and it's the liberating aspect of the hand-held camera that I like.

LOVING ACTORS TO THE POINT OF JEALOUSY

A few years ago, everybody would have told you that I was the worst director of actors in the whole industry. And everyone might have been right, although I will say in my defense that it was the kind of films I made which caused that. In a film like *Element of Crime*, for instance, it was necessary that the actors just stand there and say nothing, or that their behavior appear a little mechanical. In films like this one, the setting was more important than the actors, really. But now my ap-proach has changed. I try to put more life into my films. And I guess my technique as a director has improved a little also. I realize the best way to get something from actors is to give them freedom. Give them freedom and encourage them, that's all I can say. It's like everything else in life: if you want something done well, you have to be extremely positive about it and about people's ability to accomplish it.

In the beginning of my career, I saw a documentary about the way Ingmar Bergman directed his actors. After each take, he would go to his cast and say, "Oh, that was great! Beautiful! Fantastic! Maybe you could improve this a little, but really . . . marvelous!" And I remember I wanted to throw up. It felt so exaggerated and overdone and . . . well, it seemed fake to the cynical young filmmaker that I was. But today, I've come to realize he was right, that it is the right approach. You have to encourage actors, you have to support them. And let's not be afraid of the cliché: you have to love them. Really. I know that on a film like *The Idiots*, for instance, I came to love my actors so much that I became extremely jealous. Because they had developed this very close relationship amongst themselves, they had created a sort of community from which I felt excluded. It couldn't have lasted very much longer, because at the end, I was getting so upset that I didn't want to work anymore. I was pouting like a child because I was jealous. I felt like they were all having fun and I had to work, like they were all kids and I had to be the teacher.

EVOLVING, NOT IMPROVING

It's important for a director to evolve, but most people mistake evolution with improvement, and these are two different things. I have evolved in my work because I have always moved toward different things. But I don't feel I have improved. And I'm not trying to sound humble when I say that. On the contrary, really, because—and it might be unbearable to hear—my only gift as a director is that I am always completely sure of what I am doing. I was sure of myself when I was in film school, I was sure of myself when I made my first film . . . I've never been in doubt when it comes to my work. Of course, I might have been in doubt of how people would react to it, but I never doubted what I wanted to do. I've never wanted to improve, and I don't think I have. But I've worked and I've changed. And I never had fear in what I was doing. When I see the way a lot of other directors work, you can tell there's a certain amount of fear in connection to their work. But that's a limitation that I couldn't accept. I have many fears in my private life, many. But not in my work. If that happened, I would stop working immediately.

Films: *Nocturne* (1981), *Pictures of a Liberation* (1982), *The Element of Crime* (1984), *Epidemic* (1987), *Medea* (1988), *Zentropa (Europa)* (1991), *Breaking the Waves* (1996), *The Idiots* (1998), *Dancer in the Dark* (2000)

WONG KAR-WAI
b. 1958, Shanghai, China

When Hong Kong cinema finally reached Western audiences in the late eighties, its style was quickly and correctly categorized as a strictly commercial approach to filmmaking. Wong Kar-wai's arrival changed everything. With the same visual tools that his peers were using to make action blockbusters, Wong started making very personal and extremely poetic films, disregarding the rules of narrative storytelling and challenging traditional Chinese mores. Few of his contemporaries have dared tackle homosexuality as directly as he did in Happy Together. From the dizzying Chungking Express to the hypnotizing In the Mood for Love, Wong's work is incredibly modern and particularly powerful. After seeing In the Mood for Love, a critic friend of mine wrote, "I never thought I could be so moved by a film that does not have a story." The remark sums it up rather well.

Wong Kar-wai is something of an enigma. He cultivates a mysterious image of himself, with sunglasses that he never—ever—takes off, and a style of answering questions in very short sentences that prevents him from ever letting out too much, at least with journalists. As a result, his master class is probably one of the briefest interviews I did for this collection. However, Wong Kar-wai's enigmatic answers were so surprising in so many respects, and so thoughtful, that they made up for his terseness.

▪ Master Class with Wong Kar-wai

The reason I went into filmmaking had more to do with geography than anything else. I was born in Shanghai, but my parents moved to Hong Kong when I was five years old. People in Hong Kong don't speak the same dialect as people in Shanghai, so I was not able to talk with people there; I couldn't make any friends. And my mother, who was in the same situation, often took me to the movies because it was something that could be understood beyond words. It was a universal language based on images.

Like a lot of people in my generation, therefore, I discovered the world through films and later on through TV. Twenty years earlier, I might have chosen to express myself through songs. Fifty years earlier, it might have been books. But I grew up with images, and it felt rather natural for me to go and study visuals. I got into graphic design because in those days there was no film school in Hong Kong. People who wanted to study cinema had to go to Europe or the United States. I couldn't afford to. But I was lucky enough to come out of school at a time when all the young people who had gone abroad to study film were coming back to Hong Kong and were trying to create a new wave of artists. So I worked in television for one year, and then I became a writer for movies and did that for ten years before I started directing. *In the Mood for Love* is my tenth film. And yet, if you asked me, I think I wouldn't really consider myself a director. I still see myself as an audience member—an audience member who stepped behind a camera. When I make a film, I always try to reproduce the first impressions that I had as a film lover. And I believe I make films for the audience, first and foremost. But there has to be more than that, of course. It's not the only reason. It must only be *one* of the reasons. The rest is more personal and, well, more secret.

THE PLACE COMES BEFORE THE STORY

I write my own scripts. It's not a matter of ego; it's not a question of being the "author" of the film . . . Frankly, my biggest dream is to wake up in the morning and have a script waiting for me on my bedside table. But until that happens, I guess I'll have to write. Writing is not an easy job, though. It's not an enjoyable experience. I've tried working with writers, but I always felt that writers seemed to have a problem working with a director who was also a writer. I don't quite know why, but we always got into conflict. So eventually, I decided that if I could write my own scripts, why bother with writers?

I have to say, however, that I have a rather unusual approach to screenwriting. You see, I write as a director, not as a writer. So I write with images. And to me, the most important thing about the script is to know the space it takes place in. Because if you know that, then you can decide what the characters do in this space. The space even tells you who the characters are, why they're there, and so on. Everything else just comes bit by bit if you have a place in your mind. So I have to scout locations before I even start writing. Also, I always start with a lot of ideas, but the story itself is never clear. I know what I don't want, but I don't know exactly what I want. I think the whole process of making a film is actually a way for me to find all these answers. And until I have found the answers, I'll continue to make the film. Sometimes I find the answers on the set, sometimes during the editing, sometimes three months after the first screening.

The only thing that I try to make very clear when I start a film is the genre that I want to place it in. As a kid, I grew up watching genre movies, and I was fascinated by all the different genres, such as Westerns, ghost stories, swashbucklers . . . So I try to make each of my films in a different genre. And I think that's part of what has made them so original. *In the*

Mood for Love, for example, is a story about two people, and it could easily have been very boring. But instead of treating it as a love story, I decided to approach it like a thriller, like a suspense movie. These two people start out as victims, and then they start to investigate, to try to understand how things happened. This is the way I structured this film, with very short scenes and an attempt to create constant tension. That's probably what made it so surprising to the audience, which was expecting a classic love story.

MUSIC IS A COLOR

Music is very important in my films. Yet I rarely have music composed for my films because I find it very hard to communicate with musicians. They have a musical language; I have a visual one. Most of the time we can't understand each other. Yet film music must be visual. It has to have a chemistry that works with the image. So the way I work this out is that whenever I hear music that inspires something visual for me, I record it and put it aside, knowing that I will use it later on.

I use music during all stages of the film process. Of course, I use it when I'm editing. And one thing I particularly like to do is use period music in contemporary films. Because music is like a color. It is like a filter that tints everything in a different shade. And I find that using music from another time than the one in which the image is set makes everything a little more ambiguous, a little more complex. I also use music on the set—less to create a mood than to find a rhythm, though. When I try to explain to a camera operator the speed I want for a certain move, a piece of music will often communicate it better than a thousand words.

INVENT YOUR OWN LANGUAGE

I'm not particularly obsessed with technical things. To me, the camera is nothing more than a tool used to translate what the eye sees. Yet when I arrive on the set for a given scene, I always start with the frame because I have to know the space the scene is going to evolve in. It's only once I know that that I can decide the blocking of the actors. I explain what I want to the director of photography; we've worked together so much that it usually requires very little talk. I give him the angle, he frames it, and nine times out of ten, I'm happy. He knows me so well that if I say "a close-up," he knows exactly how close I mean.

As a rule, I don't cover much. It depends on the scene, of course. Very often there's only one way to shoot it. But in some scenes, and especially if the scene is something of a transition, where the story can shift from one point of view to another, then I will do a lot of coverage because it is only in the editing that I will be able to know whether the story should follow this person or that person. As for deciding where to set the camera in a given shot, well . . . there is grammar, and yet it is always an experiment. You always have to ask yourself the question "Why? Why do I put the camera here, why not there?" There must be a sort of logic, even if it means nothing to anyone else but you. It's like poetry, really. Poets use words in different ways, sometimes for the sound, for the tone, for the meaning, and so on. Everyone can create a different language with the same elements. But ultimately, it has to mean something. This may sound analytical, but it's not.

Most of my decisions are instinctive. I usually have a strong feeling of what's right and what's not, and it's as simple as that. Film is a difficult thing to analyze verbally anyway. It's very much like food. When you have a flavor lingering in your mouth, you cannot explain or describe that flavor correctly to someone else. It is very abstract. It's the same with film. And in fact, I haven't really changed in my way of working since I began. That's too bad, because I don't think it's a good way of working. But unfortunately, it is the only way I know. I always wanted to be like Hitchcock, who decided everything before he shot. But somehow I can't work like that, so, well, too bad.

One last thing: to be a director, you have to be honest. Not with other people, but with yourself. You have to know why you're making a film; you have to know when you're making a mistake and not put the blame on others.

Films: *As Tears Go By* (1988), *Days of Being Wild* (1990), *Chungking Express* (1994), *Ashes of Time* (1994), *Fallen Angels* (1995), *The Buenos Aires Affair (Happy Together)* (1997), *In the Mood for Love* (2000)

IN A CLASS BY HIMSELF

Jean-Luc Godard

Of all the directors in this book, Jean-Luc Godard is the one who started making films the earliest, in 1961. At the same time, he is possibly the most modern and innovative of them all. In any case, it seemed impossible to include him in any of the other sections. And I think all the other directors will agree that he has a place of his own in the history of film-making.

JEAN-LUC GODARD
b. 1930, Paris, France

When I was a teenager, I thought Jean-Luc Godard embodied everything I felt was wrong with French cinema. I loved Hollywood movies because they had beautiful shots, attractive stars, and entertaining plots. Here was Godard making films his own way, which was exactly the opposite. It took me some time to understand why so many people talked about him with awe.

Ironically, it was as a student at NYU that I finally began to understand how Godard and the other directors of the New Wave had revolutionized cinema, opening the door for a whole new approach to making films. Though it is true that contemporary French directors have been struggling ever since to find a way out of the New Wave, its impact on cinema is immeasurable. Godard's Breathless (A bout de souffle), Crazy Pete (Pierrot le fou), and Contempt (Le mépris) are lessons in themselves for any aspiring filmmaker.

But that was forty years ago. Today, Jean-Luc Godard makes films that very few people go to see. If they do, they rarely understand them. Nevertheless, I've almost never met anyone who matched so closely the profile of what I figured a true genius would be like. The interview (which I conducted with Studio editor Christophe D'Yvoire) had been planned to last an hour, but ended up lasting three because Godard had so much to say. I must confess, though, that there were several moments during our conversation when I thought to myself, "Gee, this sounds fascinating, but what in the world is he talking about?"

▪ Master Class with Jean-Luc Godard

I have often been asked to teach cinema, and I have generally refused because the idea of teaching the way it is usually done—meaning, to screen a film and then discuss it with a class—is an unpleasant one, even a shocking one as far as I am concerned. Cinema has to be discussed while you watch it. You have to talk about something concrete, about an actual picture that's in front of you. In most of the film classes I have attended, I think the students see nothing: they see what they are being told they just saw.

In 1990, however, I did sign a contract with the FEMIS [the French National Film School] to set up my own production office inside the school. My idea was to create something that already exists in biology departments, for example: a sort of "live" lab, a place where students could observe how things are really done. I would have shown them every step, from writing scripts to dealing with producers, preparation, editing, everything.

It would have been a completely practical way of learning. Take medicine, for instance: you don't show med students a guy with an ear infection, then send the guy home and tell the students, "You have just seen someone with an ear infection; now I will *tell* you how to cure it." That would be ridiculous. You have to perform the whole thing on the patient, in front of the students—otherwise it's pointless. Well, I think it's the same thing with cinema. And that is what I wanted to do. It seemed a less theoretical—and a less terrorizing—way of teaching than the usual. But the truth of the matter is, I think I wasn't really wanted, not even by the students. The whole project gradually fell through, and the school didn't even return my phone calls. I felt like the director Andre De Toth, when he worked under contract for Warner Bros; he explained that when you were fired, no one ever told you so.

You just showed up at the studio one morning and the locks on your office door had been changed.

LOVING CINEMA IS ALREADY LEARNING TO MAKE FILMS

The New Wave* was a particular trend in many respects, one of them being that we were children of the museum—and by that I mean the Cinémathèque.† Painters and musicians have always learned their craft in academies, where the teaching system is extremely precise, with thoroughly defined techniques. But in cinema, there were never such obvious schools or methods. And so when we discovered the Cinémathèque, which was essentially a museum of cinema, we thought, "Hey, there's something new, something no one has told us about!" I mean, my mother had talked to me about Picasso, Beethoven, and Dostoevsky, but she had never said anything about Eisenstein or Griffith. Imagine having never heard about Homer or Plato and then walking into a library and stumbling across their books . . . you'd think, "Why on earth has no one ever told me about these works!" Well, that's how we felt, and I think that amazement was our main motivation because suddenly we had discovered a whole new world. At least, we thought we had: I really think today that, in fact, cinema was just an ephemeral thing and that it was already beginning to disappear.

Going to the Cinémathèque was already a part of making films because we loved everything—two good scenes in a movie were enough for us to call it brilliant—and because we immersed ourselves in cinema. Raymond Chandler used to

*The directors who emerged in the early sixties and created the New Wave were Jean-Luc Godard, François Truffaut, Eric Rohmer, Jacques Rivette, and Louis Malle.
†The Cinémathèque Française was created by the French government to preserve, archive, restore, and exhibit as many films as possible, starting with those from the early years of cinema. It is a cross between an art theater and a museum, with a daily program of films that cannot be seen anywhere else.

say, "When you write a novel, you write it all day long, not just when you're sitting behind your typewriter. You write it as you smoke a cigarette, as you eat lunch, as you make a phone call." It's the same with cinema. I feel that I was making films even before I actually started to make them. And I probably learned more by watching films than by making them.

But then again, what does "learning" mean? The artist Eugène Delacroix often explained that he sometimes started out wanting to paint a flower, and then suddenly he'd start painting lions, crazed horsemen, and raped women. He didn't understand how or why. But then, when he finally looked back at the whole thing, he realized he actually *had* painted a flower. I think that's the way you learn. I see a lot of films where, when you reach the end, you see that the beginning is no longer a part of it—it has been forgotten, put aside as though it isn't worth anything any more. How can a director learn anything this way? I wonder.

YOU WANT TO MAKE A FILM? PICK UP A CAMERA

The advice I would give today to anyone who wants to become a director is quite simple: Make a film. In the sixties, it wasn't so easy because there wasn't even Super 8. If you wanted to shoot anything, you had to rent a 16-millimeter camera, and often it would be silent. But today, nothing is as easy as buying or borrowing a small video camera. You have a picture, you have sound, and you can screen your film on any TV set. So when an aspiring director comes to me for advice, my answer is always the same: "Take a camera, shoot something, and show it to someone. Anyone. It can be a friend, your next-door neighbor, or the grocer down the street, it doesn't matter. Show your audience what you've shot and observe their reaction. If they seem to find it interesting, then shoot something else. For instance, make a film about a typical day in your life. But find an interesting way of telling it. If the description of your day is 'I got up, shaved, had some coffee, made a phone call . . .' and on screen we actually see you getting up, shaving, having coffee, and making a phone call, you will quickly realize that this is not interesting at all. You must then think and discover what else there is in your day, which way you can show it to make it more interesting. And then you must try that. And maybe it won't work. So you'll have to think of another way. And maybe what you'll eventually realize is that you're not interested in making a film about your typical day. So make a film about something else. But ask yourself why—always ask yourself why. If you want to make a film about your girlfriend, make a film about your girlfriend. But do it completely: go to museums and look at the way the great masters painted the women they loved. Read books and see how authors talk about the women they love. Then make a film about your girlfriend. All this you can do on video. Panavision cameras, spotlights, and dollies? You'll have plenty of time to worry about that later on."

MAKING A FILM OUT OF DESIRE—OR OUT OF NEED

I think there are two ways of approaching filmmaking. The first one is that of directors who make "traditional," maybe "conventional," films, but who, at least, are consistent in their process. What I mean by that is that they start out with something that resembles desire, an idea that seduces them. That idea then starts to grow, to develop, and they start taking notes; they start seeing sets, even images, then characters and a story. Then they start preparing the film the same way an architect prepares the blueprint of a house, making sure everything will work out perfectly. After that, there's the actual shoot, which basically consists of accomplishing, as precisely and as comfortably as possible, what has been prepared on the blueprint. And eventually, there's the editing, which is the last moment of semi-freedom and invention available to the director.

As I said, that's one approach. Mine is different. It usually starts with an abstract feeling, a sort of strange attraction to something I am not sure of. And making the film is a way for me to find out what that abstract element is, to verify it. This method implies a lot of going back and forth, a lot of trial and error, a lot of instinctive changes, and it is only when the film is totally finished that I am able to discover whether my instinct was right or not. In my mind, the process is a lot like modern painting, except that in painting you can always erase what you tried out if it didn't work, or just paint over it. Film is not quite as convenient—and it's much more costly.

One thing I must explain is that I always start working on a film with the certainty that I can actually, physically, make it. What I mean by that is that I always got a green light from a producer before I wrote a single line of the script. So, of course, once that project gets going, you have to get going too. It's a little bit like a marriage: once you've taken that step, there's no turning back. You have to wake up in the morning, go to work to provide for the family, watch your expenses, plan for the future . . . it's a commitment you can't postpone. It becomes an obligation—but a particularly healthy one, I think.

DUTIES OF THE DIRECTOR

It seems to me the director has several duties—and I mean that in both the professional and moral sense of the term. One of these duties is to explore, to be in a perpetual state of research. Another one is to let himself be amazed once in a while. I am always longing to see a film that will move me tremendously, and of which I cannot possibly be jealous, because it is beautiful and I love beautiful films. A film that overwhelms me forces me to reassess my own work, because what it says to me is "This is better than what you do, so try to improve."

When I was part of the New Wave, we spent time discussing other people's films. And I remember that when we saw *Hiroshima mon amour* by Alain Resnais, we were just stunned. We thought we had discovered everything about cinema, we thought we knew it all, and suddenly we were confronted with something that had been done without us, without our knowledge, and that deeply moved us. It was as though the Soviets, in 1917, had discovered that another country had had a Communist revolution which worked as well as theirs—or even better! Imagine how they would have felt . . .

As for the third duty of the director, I think it is, very simply, to reflect on *why* he or she makes each film—and to not be satisfied with the first answer. I started making films because it was something vital; there was nothing else I could do. But when I see a lot of films today, I feel like their directors could very easily do another job. I think they believe they do what they *say* they are doing, but they aren't actually doing it. They think they have made a film about something, but they haven't.

There are two levels of content in a film: the visible and the invisible. What you put in front of the camera is the visible. And if there is nothing else, then you are making a TV movie. The real films, for me, are those where there is something invisible, which can be seen—or discerned—through the visible part, and only because the visible part has been arranged in a certain fashion. In a way, the visible is a little bit like a filter which, when put at a certain angle, allows certain rays of light to go through and allow you to see the invisible. Too many directors today do not go beyond the visible level. They should ask themselves more questions. Or critics should ask them those questions. But not after the films are made, as it is done today. No, that's too late. You have to ask the questions before the film is made, and you should ask them in the same manner as a police officer interrogates a suspect—anything less than that is worthless.

THE IMPORTANCE OF THE EXCHANGE

I think it is of primary importance for a filmmaker to be able to gather around him a group of people with whom he can communicate and, most of all, exchange ideas. When Sartre wrote something, it was the result of endless conversations with forty or fifty people. He didn't come up with all this just sitting alone in a room. I think making a film on your own is about as hard as playing tennis alone: if there isn't anyone on the other side to hit the ball back, it just can't work.

The best films are those on which there has been an exchange. And to accomplish that, the director really needs only one other person, who can be an actor or a technician. Today, however, I feel that I am having more and more trouble finding people like that on the films I make. The people I work with don't really seem to care; they don't seem to ask themselves too many questions, and they certainly never ask *me* any.

In one of my latest films, for instance, one of the actresses says the following line: "Acting kills the text." This is a line by Marguerite Duras that I don't necessarily agree with—I put it there more as a question than as a statement. However, what really surprised me is that the young actress who said this line never asked me what it meant or why I was asking her to say it. We would have discussed it, and I'm sure that eventually it would have been a better scene for it. I am having more and more trouble finding people who are actually interested in making films. The only one with whom I still have any sort of dialogue is the producer, because he has an obvious interest in the film. It may be a financial one, but it's better than nothing. Most of the others make me feel like I'm the promiscuous girl of the village—you know, the one the young boys sleep with so they can brag about it.

This was certainly the case with Delon.* He "slept with" Godard so he could then go to the Cannes Film Festival and climb the big red-carpeted stairway. This was the deal, actually. This was pretty much our agreement: "Let's not fight; I get to make my film and you get to climb the big stairway." Well, he got what he wanted. But now he feels he has to say bad things about the film. I think that's a shame.

DIRECTING ACTORS IS LIKE TRAINING ATHLETES

I have never agreed with the concept of actors being able to make you believe they are the characters they play. The ultimate example of that is probably the Chekhov play in which the actress is supposed to pretend she is a seagull. A lot of people accept it. I don't. For me, the actor plays a part; he or she isn't the part. I never really directed actors. With Anna, of course, I didn't have to worry, because she pretty much directed herself.† Otherwise, most of the time, my directions to actors rarely go beyond "Louder" or "More slowly." Sometimes I will say things like "If it doesn't ring true to you, then do it in a way that you think would ring true to me." But I often let the actors make their own creations; I let them be very free. Well, not *entirely* free: they have to follow a very specific path. But they go down this path alone, and in the manner they want. I feel that my duty toward them is mostly to give

---

*Alain Delon is one of France's biggest commercial stars. In 1990, he agreed to play the lead in Jean-Luc Godard's *New Wave* (*Nouvelle vague*).
†Anna Karina, the Danish actress with whom Jean-Luc Godard made most of his films in the sixties, and to whom he was married from 1961 to 1967.

them good working conditions: a nice set, a nice frame, good lighting, and so on.

I am totally unable to accomplish the kind of deep, intense directorial work that people like Bergman, Cukor, or Renoir did. I mean, you can tell these directors really loved their actors, in the same way that some painters loved their models. I think the good actors' directors are those who have a very definite idea of what they want, who are lucky enough to be working with the right actor for that part, and who are both very firm and very tolerant toward that actor, the way a good coach might be in sports. You have to push your actors, to make them work as hard as they can, because they need it (even if some don't like it), and at the same time, you have to do it with a light, pleasant, and friendly hand, which I'm afraid I was never able to do. I fear I have often been way too heavy-handed with actors, mostly because I was too busy working on a dozen other things at the same time.

MOVING THE CAMERA FOR THE SAKE OF IT IS A MISTAKE

Finding where to put the camera in a given scene is a hard task: there are really no rules, no principles you can rely on. One thing I have noticed, however, is that if I really don't know where to put the camera, it usually means that something else is wrong: the scene isn't good, the actors' blocking isn't good, the dialogue doesn't work . . . It works like a sort of alarm, a warning mechanism. There are no rules you can rely on as to either when or how to move the camera. It is something you decide instinctively, the same way a painter suddenly decides to use the color blue instead of the color red. But, once again, you have to ask yourself why you do it.

Often when I see camera movement in films today, I think of a line by Cocteau: "Why dolly along a moving horse, since it makes it look like it's standing still?" I have a feeling most directors today move the camera because they have seen it moving in other films. Now, this is something that, in a way, I have done myself to a certain extent. But I did it in a totally conscious and deliberate way: I copied a Douglas Sirk dolly move the same way a young painter copies the work of a master, as practice. But today it looks like a lot of the young directors move the camera to make their films look "cinematic." They look like they're not quite certain why they frame this way or why they move this way—and it doesn't seem to particularly bother them. In many ways, it reminds me of certain operas, where most of the effects are there not to help the story but to offer a distraction because the story is boring.

Max Ophuls probably created some of the most beautiful camera moves. They were long, uncut, both instinctive and extremely well thought out, totally self-managed. Orson Welles also did beautiful camera moves. Sure, his were more of a tour de force, but cinema also is about virtuosity. I once wanted to do things like that. In *New Wave* (*Nouvelle vague*), for instance, I raised the dolly tracks to the height of the trees. In my last film, however, I did not move the camera at all. Maybe it is because when I see all those who move it without reason, I feel a certain need for abstention.

THE DANGER OF WANTING TO BE AN AUTEUR

One of the negative legacies of the New Wave is certainly the perverting of the auteur theory. It used to be that the authors of the films were the writers—a tradition that was derived from literature. If you look at the credits of old films, the names of the directors came last, except for people like Capra or Ford, but only because they also were producers of their films. Then we came in and said, "No, the director is the real founder and creator of the film. And in that sense, Hitchcock is as much an author as Tolstoy." From there, we developed the auteur theory, which consisted of supporting the author, even when he was weak. It was easier for us to support a bad film made by an author than a good film made by someone who was not an author.

But then the whole idea became perverted; it was transformed into a cult of the author instead of a cult of the author's work. So everybody became an author, and today even the set decorators want to be recognized as the "authors" of the nails they put into the walls. The term "auteur" hence does not really mean anything anymore. Very few films are made by their authors today. Too many people try to do things they can't possibly achieve. There are talents, there are people with originality, but the system we created doesn't exist anymore. It has become a vast swamp. I think the problem was that when we created the auteur theory, we insisted on the word "auteur," whereas it's the word "theory" we should have insisted upon because the real goal of this concept was not to show *who* makes a good film but to demonstrate *what* makes a good film.

Films: *Breathless (A bout de souffle)* (1960), *A Woman Is a Woman (Une femme est une femme)* (1961), *My Life to Live (Vivre sa vie)* (1962), *The Little Soldier (Le petit soldat)* (1963), *Les carabiniers* (1963), *Contempt (Le mépris)* (1963), *Band of Outsiders (Bande à part)* (1964), *A Married Woman (Une femme mariée)* (1964), *Alphaville* (1965), *Crazy Pete (Pierrot le fou)* (1965), *Masculine-Feminine (Masculin-féminin)* (1966), *Made in U.S.A.* (1966), *Two or Three Things I Know About Her (Deux ou trois choses que je sais d'elle)* (1967), *La Chinoise* (1967), *Weekend* (1967), *A Film Like Any Other (Un film comme les autres)* (1968), *The Joy of Knowledge (Le gai savoir)* (1968), *East Wind (Le vent d'est)* (1969), *Vladimir and Rosa (Vladimir et Rosa)* (1970), *Pravda* (1970), *All's Well (Tout va bien)* (1972), *Number 2 (Numéro 2)* (1975),

How's It Going? (Comment ça va?) (1976), *Here and Elsewhere (Ici et ailleurs)* (1976), *Every Man for Himself (Sauve qui peut la vie)* (1979), *Godard's Passion (Passion)* (1982), *First Name: Carmen (Prénom : Carmen)* (1984), *Hail Mary (Je vous salue Marie)* (1985), *Detective* (1985), *Keep Up Your Right (Soigne ta droite)* (1987), *King Lear* (1987), *New Wave (Nouvelle vague)* (1990), *Alas for Me (Hélas pour moi)* (1993), *For Ever Mozart* (1996), *In Praise of Love (Eloge de l'amour)* (2001)

Photo Credits